Meeting SEN
in the Curriculum:
CITIZENSHIP

Other titles in the Meeting Special Needs in the Curriculum series:

Meeting Special Needs in English
Tim Hurst
1 84312 157 3

Meeting Special Needs in Maths
Brian Sharp
1 84312 158 1

Meeting Special Needs in Modern Foreign Languages
Sally McKeown
1 84312 165 4

Meeting Special Needs in Religious Education
Dilwyn Hunt
1 84312 167 0

Meeting Special Needs in History
Richard Harris and Ian Luff
1 84312 163 8

Meeting Special Needs in Design and Technology
Louise Davies
1 84312 166 2

Meeting Special Needs in Art
Kim Earle and Gill Curry
1 84312 161 1

Meeting Special Needs in Music
Victoria Jacquiss and Diane Paterson
1 84312 168 9

Meeting Special Needs in ICT
Mike North and Sally McKeown
1 84312 160 3

Meeting Special Needs in Science
Carol Holden
1 84312 159 X

Meeting Special Needs in Geography
Diane Swift
1 84312 162 X

Meeting Special Needs in P.E/Sports Studies
Crispin Andrews
1 84312 164 6

Meeting SEN
in the Curriculum:
CITIZENSHIP

Alan Combes

 David Fulton Publishers

David Fulton Publishers Ltd
The Chiswick Centre, 414 Chiswick High Road, London W4 5TF

www.fultonpublishers.co.uk

First published in Great Britain in 2004 by David Fulton Publishers

10 9 8 7 6 5 4 3 2 1

Note: the right of Alan Combes to be identified as the author of this work has been asserted by him in accordance with the Copyright, Designs and Patents Act 1988.

Copyright © Alan Combes 2004

British Library Cataloguing in Publication Data
A catalogue record for this book is available from the British Library.

David Fulton Publishers is a division of Granada Learning, part of ITV plc.

ISBN 1 84312 169 7

Typeset by Servis Filmsetting Ltd, Manchester
Printed and bound in Great Britain

Contents

Foreword   vii
Contributors to the Series   ix
Contents of the CD   xii

Introduction   1

1.   Meeting Special Educational Needs – Your Responsibility   5

2.   Departmental Policy   12
     Where to start when writing a policy   15
     The content of an SEN departmental policy   15
     General statement with reference to the school's SEN policy   15
     Definition of SEN   15
     Provision for staff within the department   16
     Provision for pupils with SEN   17
     Resources and learning materials   18
     Staff qualifications and continuing professional development needs   18
     Monitoring and reviewing the policy   19

3.   Different Types of SEN   20
     Asperger's Syndrome   22
     Attention Deficit Disorder (with or without hyperactivity) (ADD/ADHD)   23
     Autistic Spectrum Disorders (ASD)   24
     Behavioural, emotional and social development needs   25
     Behavioural, emotional, social difficulty (BESD)   26
     Cerebral palsy (CP)   27
     Down's Syndrome (DS)   28
     Fragile X Syndrome   29
     Moderate learning difficulties (MLD)   30
     Physical disability (PD)   31
     Semantic Pragmatic Disorder (SPD)   32
     Sensory impairments   33
     Hearing impairment (HI)   33
     Visual impairment (VI)   34
     Multi-sensory impairment   35
     Severe learning difficulties (SLD)   36
     Profound and multiple learning difficulties (PMLD)   37
     Specific learning difficulties (SpLD)   38
         Dyslexia   38
         Dyscalculia   39
         Dyspraxia   40
     Speech, language and communication difficulties (SLCD)   41
     Tourette's Syndrome (TS)   42

4. **The Inclusive Citizenship Classroom**   43
    Why PSHE and citizenship are particularly suited to inclusive education   43
    An important difference between PSHE and citizenship   44
    Some challenges inherent in an inclusive approach to PSHE and
        citizenship   45
    Realistic demands in terms of language and understanding   46
    How school atmosphere and events can support an active curriculum   49
    Display as a tool for inclusion   50
    Bearing inclusion in mind when choosing appropriate textbooks   51
    How classroom layout can maximise the positive effects of inclusion   52
    Overcoming the problems of storing records and data   53
    The use of ICT to support an inclusive policy in citizenship   54
    Extra-curricular activities and inclusion   55

5. **Teaching and Learning Styles**   57
    What makes citizenship and PSHE unique   57
    How citizenship is organised in the original Parliamentary orders   57
    An active approach to becoming informed citizens   58
    Teaching 'rights and responsibilities' to an inclusive class   59
    Setting an appropriate homework assignment   62
    Teaching about diversity in a way which promotes inclusion   62
    Profile questions   63
    Considering diversity of language as a citizenship project   64
    Introducing the idea of cultural diversity   65
    Implications of practical work in citizenship for pupils with SEN   66
    How to use research and the internet as a basis for homework   66
    How the citizenship curriculum can have a bearing on the whole school   67
    Working arrangements in class   69
    Modelling social skills   69
    Linking performance management to citizenship/PSHE teaching   70

6. **Monitoring and Assessment**   71
    What Ofsted says about monitoring citizenship   71
    Including pupils with learning difficulties in PSHE and citizenship   75
    Developing a method of self-reporting for all pupils in citizenship   79
    When it is impossible to match a pupil with an end of key stage
        description   82
    The role of citizenship and PSHE in the IEP process   84

7. **Managing Support**   86
    What makes pupil support in PSHE and citizenship so valuable   86
    Helping the TA cope with the demands of secondary PSHE   87
    Helping the TA cope with the demands of secondary citizenship   88
    The most important aspects of a supportive role   88
    The importance of the TA's role in monitoring and assessing citizenship   90
    The relationship between PSHE/citizenship departments and their TAs   91
    Helping the TA to develop their abilities in PSHE and citizenship   92

Appendices   94
References   142
Further Reading   143

Foreword

At a recent conference on citizenship for teachers, co-ordinators and advisers, David Kerr (NFER and former Professional Officer to the Crick Advisory Group) reflected on the two years since citizenship had become a statutory subject of the curriculum in English schools. He referred to us as being at 'the start of a long stage in developing citizenship in schools' Alan Combes' book is both timely and apposite in reaffirming the original principles of the Crick Report (1998) in showing how these principles can be practically implemented as an entitlement for all pupils.

During the course of this text the author demonstrates that 'education through citizenship can be the most enabling and empowering perspective for pupils with SEN' (DfES National CPD Strategy for Citizenship, 2004). My own, and CSV's, experience of developing active citizenship with pupils over the last ten years bears out this observation: the opportunity for pupils to choose, plan and develop their own school–community projects can be a life-changing experience. Group activities, where all pupils are involved in trying out roles, can help them to develop important skills for life, work and citizenship. Such groups work to particular advantage where pupils with SEN are integrated with 'mainstream' peers and their experiences as well as their vision are blended to mutual advantage.

Inclusion, and how this can be achieved through the teaching and learning of citizenship, lies at the heart of this book. Whilst the pivotal and influential role of the SENCO is highlighted, all teachers need to be involved, and training time for whole staff initiatives is recommended.

Alan Combes' belief is that the ambition of pupils with SEN should be realised through their 'taking greater responsibility for acts of citizenship within the school and the wider community'. 'Participation', 'concrete experiences' and 'management of own learning' are the glue which help these ambitions to be secured. The author provides rich and challenging examples for teachers, showing how all pupils can achieve according to their abilities and varying modes of communication.

Combes cautions against under-estimating the capabilities of students with learning difficulties in citizenship. The Salisbury Project (DfES/CSV 2003) provided evidence that pupils with a wide range of SEN were able to model effective practice for their peers in work-related learning and enterprise education.

This book will provide both practical support and reassurance to teachers getting to grips with the challenges of monitoring and assessing citizenship. The case studies (in the Appendices) provide a valuable tool for showing how pupils can be enabled to be effective, as well as active, citizens. The implementation of citizenship has been described frequently as 'a marathon rather than a sprint'.

Foreword

This book will take a lot of the pain out of that marathon and hasten the goal of all pupils achieving their rightful place as genuinely empowered citizens.

Peter Hayes, Director
CSV Education for Citizenship
September 2004

Contributors to the Series

Meeting SEN in Citizenship

The author (and series editor)

Alan Combes began teaching in 1967 and started writing for the *TES* in 1980. He authored a regular column looking at good citizenship practice in secondary schools across the country for the *TES* in 1999–2000. He has run whole-school training sessions in PSHE and citizenship as well as working for several LEAs in a similar capacity. He has been used as an adviser and author by the DfES and as a speaker by NASEN. He has written citizenship text books for Key Stages 3 and 4 – *21st Century Citizen* – which are published by Cable Educational. He has recently taught citizenship at the Caedmon School in Whitby.

A dedicated team of SEN specialists and subject specialists have contributed to the *Meeting Special Needs in the Curriculum* series.

SEN specialists

Sue Briggs is a freelance education consultant based in Hereford. She writes and speaks on inclusion, special educational needs and disability, and Autistic Spectrum Disorders and is a lay member of the SEN and Disability Tribunal. Until recently, she was SEN Inclusion Co-ordinator for Herefordshire Education Directorate. Originally trained as a secondary music teacher, Sue has extensive experience in mainstream and special schools. For six years she was teacher in charge of a language disorder unit.

Sue Cunningham is a Learning Support Co-ordinator at a large mainstream secondary school in the West Midlands where she manages a large team of Learning Support teachers and assistants. She has experience of working in both mainstream and special schools and has set up and managed a resource base for pupils with moderate learning difficulties in the mainstream as part of an initiative to promote a more inclusive education for pupils with SEN.

Sally McKeown has responsibility for language-based work in the Inclusion team at Becta. She has a particular interest in learning difficulties and dyslexia. She wrote the MFL Special Needs Materials for CILT's NOF training and is author of *Unlocking Potential* and co-author of *Supporting Children with Dyslexia* (Questions Publishing). She writes regularly for the *TES, Guardian* and *Special Children* magazine).

Subject specialists

Maths

Brian Sharp is a Key Stage 3 Mathematics consultant for Herefordshire. Brian has a long experience of working both in special and mainstream schools as a teacher of mathematics. He has a range of management experience, including SENCO, mathematics and ICT co-ordinator.

English

Tim Hurst has been a special educational needs co-ordinator in five schools and is particularly interested in the role and use of language in teaching.

Science

Carol Holden works as a science teacher and assistant SENCO in a mainstream secondary school. She has developed courses for pupils with SEN within science and has gained a graduate diploma and MA in Educational Studies, focusing on SEN.

History

Richard Harris has been teaching since 1989. He has taught in three comprehensive schools, as history teacher, Head of Department and Head of Faculty. He has also worked as teacher consultant for secondary history in West Berkshire.

Ian Luff is assistant headteacher of Kesgrave High School, Suffolk and has been Head of History in three comprehensive schools.

Modern foreign languages

Sally McKeown has responsibility for language-based work in the inclusion team at Becta. She wrote the MFL Special Needs Materials for CILT's NOF training and writes regularly for the *TES*, *Guardian* and *Special Children* magazines.

Design and technology

Louise T. Davies is Principal Officer for Design and Technology at the Qualifications and Curriculum Authority and also a freelance consultant. She is an experienced presenter and author of award-winning resources and books for schools. She chairs the Special Needs Advisory Group for the Design and Technology Association.

Religious education

Dilwyn Hunt has worked as a specialist RE adviser, first in Birmingham and, currently, in Dudley. He has a wide range of experience in the teaching of RE, including mainstream and special RE.

Music

Victoria Jaquiss is SEN Specialist for Music for children with emotional and behavioural difficulties in Leeds. She devised a system of musical notation primarily for use with steel pans, for which, in 2002, she was awarded the fellowship of the Royal Society of Arts.

Diane Paterson works as an inclusive music curriculum teacher in Leeds.

Geography

Diane Swift is a project leader for the Geographical Association. Her interest in special needs developed whilst she was a Staffordshire geography adviser and inspector.

PE and sport

Crispin Andrews is an education/sports writer with nine years' experience of teaching and sports coaching.

Art

Kim Earle is Able Pupils Consultant for St Helens and has been a Head of art and design. Kim is also a practising designer jeweller.

Gill Curry is Gifted and Talented Strand Co-ordinator for the Wirral. She has twenty years' experience as Head of art and has also been an art advisory teacher. She is also a practising artist specialising in print.

ICT

Mike North works for ICTC, an independent consultancy specialising in the effective use of ICT in education. He develops educational materials and provides advice and support for the SEN sector.

Sally McKeown is an education officer with Becta, the government-funded agency responsible for managing the National Grid for Learning and the FERL website. She is responsible for the use of IT for learners with disabilities, learining difficulties or additional needs.

Contents of the CD

Fig 4.1   producing your own materials
Mugger, 5 is too young to be prosecuted
Profile questions
London children share more than 300 languages
Table 7.1   Guidelines for TAs

Appendices:

1.1   What do we really think?

2.1   SENDA

3.1   Keeping strategies in mind

4.1   The responsibility of being a dog owner

4.2   Key words for Citizenship

4.3a   Y7 lesson – being a good and active citizen

4.3b   Y9 Lesson – My future

4.4   Pupils on the Reception desk – jobs itinerary

4.5   Lesson ideas for developing empathy

5.1   Differentiating between rights and responsibilities

5.2   A Questions itinerary for the story 'Mugger 5, too young to be prosecuted'.

5.3   Homework

5.4   An activity sheet for 'London children share more than 300 languages'.

5.5   Activity sheet for creating a fictional teenager

6.1   Secondary case studies

Ashraf   Cerebral Palsy

Ryan   PMLD

Sarah   Asperger's syndrome

Charlene   Williams syndrome

Matthew   ASD

Jenny   Down's syndrome

Megan   Wheelchair user

Steven   Behaviour difficulties

6.2   Individual education plans (Ashraf, Steven, Megan)

6.3   Care action plan

7.1   Assisting TA input in a citizenship discussion lesson

Introduction

All children have the right to a good education and the opportunity to fulfil their potential. All teachers should expect to teach children with special educational needs (SEN) and all schools should play their part in educating children from the local community, whatever their background or ability. (*Removing Barriers to Acheivement: The Government's Strategy for SEN*, Feb. 2004)

A raft of legislation and statutory guidance over the past few years has sought to make our mainstream education system more inclusive and ensure that pupils with a diverse range of ability and need are well catered for. This means that all staff need to have an awareness of how children learn and develop in different ways and an understanding of how barriers to achievement can be removed – or at least minimised.

These barriers often result from inappropriate teaching styles, inaccessible teaching materials or ill-advised grouping of pupils, as much as from an individual child's physical, sensory or cognitive impairments: a fact which is becoming better understood. It is this developing understanding that is now shaping the legislative and advisory landscape of our education system, and making it necessary for all teachers to reconsider carefully their curriculum planning and classroom practice.

The major statutory requirements and non-statutory guidance are summarised in Chapter 1, setting the context for this resource and providing useful starting points for departmental INSET.

It is clear that provision for pupils with special educational needs is not the sole responsibility of the Special Eductional Needs Co-ordinator (SENCO) and his/her team of assistants. If, in the past, subject teachers have 'taken a back seat' in the planning and delivery of a suitable curriculum for these children and expected the Learning Support department to bridge the gap between what was on offer in the classroom and what they actually needed – they can no longer do so. The Code of Practice (2002) states:

All teaching and non teaching staff should be involved in the development of the school's SEN policy and be fully aware of the school's procedure for identifying, assessing and making provision for pupils with SEN.

Chapter 2 looks at departmental policy for SEN provision and provides useful audit material for reviewing and developing current practice.

The term 'special educational needs' is now widely used and has become something of a catch-all descriptor – rendering it less than useful in many cases. Before the Warnock Report (1978) and subsequent introduction of the term 'special educational needs', any pupils who, for whatever reason, (cognitive difficulties, emotional and behavioural difficulties, speech and language disorders) progressed more slowly than the 'norm' were designated 'remedials' and grouped together in the bottom sets, without the benefit, in many cases, of specialist subject teachers.

But the SEN tag was also applied to pupils in special schools who had more significant needs, and had previously been identified as 'disabled' or even 'uneducable'. Add to these the deaf pupils, those with impaired vision, others with mobility problems, and even children from other countries, with a limited understanding of the English language – who may or may not have been highly intelligent – and you have a recipe for confusion to say the least.

The day-to-day descriptors used in the staffroom are gradually being moderated and refined as greater knowledge and awareness of special needs is built up. (We still hear staff describing pupils as 'totally thick', a 'nutcase' or 'complete moron' – but hopefully only as a means of letting off steam!) However, there are terms in common use which, though more measured and well-meaning, can still be unhelpful and misleading. Teachers will describe a child as being 'dyslexic' when they mean that he is poor at reading and writing; 'ADHD' has become a synonym for badly behaved; and a child who seems to be withdrawn or just eccentric is increasingly described as 'autistic'.

The whole process of applying labels is fraught with danger, but sharing a common vocabulary – and more importantly, a common understanding – can help colleagues to express their concerns about a pupil and address the issues as they appear in the classroom. Often, this is better achieved by identifying the particular areas of difficulty experienced by the pupil rather than by puzzling over what syndrome he may have. The Code of Practice identifies four main areas of difficulty and these are detailed in Chapter 3 – along with an 'at a glance' guide to a wide range of syndromes and conditions, and guidance on how they might present barriers to learning.

There is no doubt that the number of children with special needs being educated in mainstream schools is growing:

> … because of the increased emphasis on the inclusion of children with SEN in mainstream schools the number of these children is increasing, as are the severity and variety of their SEN. Children with a far wider range of learning difficulties and variety of medical conditions, as well as sensory difficulties and physical disabilities, are now attending mainstream classes. The implication of this is that mainstream school teachers need to expand their knowledge and skills with regard to the needs of children with SEN.
> (Stakes and Hornby 2000:3)

The continuing move to greater inclusion means that all teachers can now expect to teach pupils with varied and quite significant special educational needs at some time. Even five years ago, it was rare to come across children with Asperger's/Down's/Tourette's Syndrome, Autistic Spectrum Disorder or significant physical/sensory disabilities in community secondary schools. Now, they are entering mainstream education in growing numbers and there is a realisation that their 'inclusion' cannot be simply the responsibility of the SENCO and support staff. All staff have to be aware of particular learning needs and able to employ strategies that directly address those needs.

Chapter 4 considers the components of an inclusive citizenship classroom and how the physical environment and resources, structure of the lesson and teaching approaches can make a real difference to pupils with special needs. This theme is extended in Chapter 5 to look more closely at teaching and learning styles and consider ways in which to help all pupils maximise their potential.

The monitoring of pupils' achievements and progress is a key factor in identifying and meeting their learning needs. Those pupils who make slower progress than their peers are often working just as hard, or even harder, but their efforts can go unrewarded. Chapter 6 addresses the importance of target setting and subsequent assessment and review in acknowledging pupils' achievements and in showing the department's effectiveness in value-added terms.

Liaising with the SENCO and support staff is an important part of every teacher's role. The SENCO's status in a secondary school often means that this teacher is part of the leadership team and influential in shaping whole-school policy and practice. Specific duties might include:

- ensuring liaison with parents and other professionals;

- advising and supporting teaching and support staff;

- ensuring that appropriate Individual Education Plans are in place;

- ensuring that relevant background information about individual children with special educational needs is collected, recorded and updated;

- making plans for future support and setting targets for improvement;

- monitoring and reviewing action taken.

The SENCO has invariably undergone training in different aspects of special needs provision and has much to offer colleagues in terms of in-house training and advice about appropriate materials to use with pupils. The SENCO should be a frequent and valuable point of reference for all staff, but is often overlooked in this capacity. The presence of the SENCO at the occasional departmental meeting can be very effective in developing teachers' skills in relation to meeting SEN, making them aware of new initiatives and methodology and sharing information about individual children.

In most schools, however, the SENCO's skills and knowledge are channelled to the chalkface via a team of Teaching or Learning Support Assistants (TAs, LSAs). These assistants can be very able and well-qualified, but very underused in the classroom.

Chapter 7 looks at how teachers can manage in-class support in a way that makes the best use of a valuable resource.

The revised regulations for SEN provision make it clear that mainstream schools are expected to provide for pupils with a wide diversity of needs, and teaching is evaluated on the extent to which all pupils are engaged and enabled to achieve. This book has been produced in response to the implications of all of this for secondary subject teachers. It has been written by a citizenship specialist with support from colleagues who have expertise within the SEN field, so that the information and guidance given is both subject specific and pedagogically sound. The book and accompanying CD provide a resource that can be used with colleagues:

- to shape departmental policy and practice for special needs provision;

- to enable staff to react with a measured response when inclusion issues arise;

- to ensure that every pupil achieves appropriately in citizenship.

CHAPTER 1

Meeting Special Educational Needs – Your Responsibility

Inclusion in education involves the process of increasing the participation of students in, and reducing their exclusion from, the cultures, curricula and communities of local schools. (*The Index for Inclusion*, 2000)

The Index for Inclusion was distributed to all maintained schools by the Department for Education and Skills and has been a valuable tool for many schools as they have worked to develop their inclusive practice. It supports schools in the review of their policies, practices and procedures, and the development of an inclusive approach and, where it has been used as part of the school improvement process – looking at inclusion in the widest sense – it has been a great success. For many people, however, the *Index* lacked any real teeth and recent legislation and non-statutory guidance is more authoritative.

The SEN and Disability Act 2001

The SEN and Disability Act 2001 (SENDA) amended the Disability Discrimination Act and created important new duties for schools. Under this Act, schools are obliged:

- to take reasonable steps to ensure that disabled pupils are not placed at a substantial disadvantage in relation to the education and other services they provide. This means they must anticipate where barriers to learning lie and take action to remove them as far as they are able;

- to plan strategically to increase the extent to which disabled pupils can participate in the curriculum, make the physical environment more accessible and ensure that written material is provided in accessible formats.

The reasonable steps taken might include:

- changing policies and practices

- changing course requirements

5

- changing the physical features of a building

- providing interpreters or other support workers

- delivering courses in alternative ways

- providing materials in other formats

Reasonable steps might, for example, mean that all pupil materials are produced in electronic form to ensure that they can easily be converted into large print, printed onto coloured paper or put into other alternative formats, such as Braille. The staff would then be anticipating 'reasonable adjustments' that might need to be made.

See Appendix 1 for an INSET activity, 'What do we really think?' and Appendix 2 for further detail on SENDA and a related INSET activity.

The Revised National Curriculum

The Revised National Curriculum (2002) emphasises the provision of effective learning opportunities for all learners, and establishes three principles for promoting inclusion:

- setting suitable learning challenges

- responding to pupils' diverse learning needs

- overcoming potential barriers to learning and assessment

The National Curriculum guidance suggests that staff may need to differentiate tasks and materials, and facilitate access to learning by:

- encouraging pupils to use all available senses and experiences

- planning for participation in all activities

- helping children to manage their behaviour, take part in learning and prepare for work

- helping pupils to manage their emotions

- giving teachers, where necessary, the discretion to teach pupils material from earlier key stages, providing consideration is given to age-appropriate learning contexts

The Qualifications and Curriculum Authority (QCA) have also introduced performance descriptions (P levels/P scales) to enable teachers to observe and record small steps of progress made by some pupils with SEN. These descriptions outline early learning and attainment for each subject in the National Curriculum, including citizenship and PSHE. They chart progress up to

NC level 1 through eight steps. The performance descriptions for P1 to P3 are common across all subjects, and outline the types and range of general performance that some pupils with learning difficulties might characteristically demonstrate. From level P4 onwards, many believe it is possible to describe performance in a way that indicates the emergence of subject-focused skills, knowledge and understanding.

The Code of Practice for Special Educational Needs

The Revised Code of Practice (implemented in 2002) describes a cyclical process of planning, target setting and review for pupils with special educational needs. It also makes clear the expectation that the vast majority of pupils with special needs will be educated in mainstream settings. Those identified as needing over and above what the school can provide from its own resources, however, are nominated for 'School Action Plus' and outside agencies will be involved in planned intervention. This may involve professionals from the Learning Support Service, a specialist teacher or therapist, or an educational psychologist, working with the school's SENCO to put together an Individual Education Plan (IEP) for the pupil. In a minority of cases (the numbers vary widely between LEAs) pupils may be assessed by a multi-disciplinary team on behalf of the local education authority, whose representatives then decide whether or not to issue a statement of SEN. This is a legally binding document detailing the child's needs and setting out the resources which should be provided. It is reviewed every year.

Fundamental Principles of the Special Needs Code of Practice

- A child with special educational needs should have their needs met.

- The special educational needs of children will normally be met in mainstream schools or settings.

- The views of the child should be sought and taken into account.

- Parents have a vital role to play in supporting their child's education.

- Children with special educational needs should be offered full access to a broad, balanced and relevant education, including an appropriate curriculum for the Foundation stage and the National Curriculum.

Ofsted

Ofsted inspectors are required to make judgements about a school's inclusion policy, and how this is translated into practice in individual classrooms. According to Ofsted (2003) the following key factors help schools to become more inclusive:

- a climate of acceptance of all pupils;

- careful preparation of placements for SEN pupils;

- availability of sufficient suitable teaching and personal support;

- widespread awareness among staff of the particular needs of SEN pupils and an understanding of the practical ways of meeting these needs in the classroom;

- sensitive allocation to teaching groups and careful curriculum modification, timetables and social arrangements;

- availability of appropriate materials and teaching aids and adapted accommodation;

- an active approach to personal and social development, as well as to learning;

- well-defined and consistently applied approaches to managing difficult behaviour;

- assessment, recording and reporting procedures which can embrace and express adequately the progress of pupils with more complex SEN who make only small gains in learning and PSD;

- involving parents/carers as fully as possible in decision-making, keeping them well informed about their child's progress and giving them as much practical support as possible;

- developing and taking advantage of training opportunities, including links with special schools and other schools.

Policy into practice

Effective teaching for pupils with special educational needs is, by and large, effective for all pupils, but as schools become more inclusive, teachers need to be able to respond to a wider range of needs. The Government's strategy for SEN (*Removing Barriers to Learning*, 2004) sets out ambitious proposals to 'help teachers expand their repertoire of inclusive skills and strategies, and plan confidently to include children with increasingly complex needs'.

In many cases, pupils' individual needs will be met through greater differentiation of tasks and materials, i.e school-based intervention as set out in the SEN Code of Practice. A smaller number of pupils may need access to specialist equipment and approaches or to alternative or adapted activities, as part of a School Action Plus programme, augmented by advice and support from external specialists. The QCA, on its website (2003) encourages teachers to take specific action to provide access to learning for pupils with special educational needs by:

(a) providing for pupils who need help with communication, language and literacy, through:

- using texts that pupils can read and understand

- using visual and written materials in different formats, including large print, symbol text and Braille

- using ICT, other technological aids and taped materials

- using alternative and augmentative communication, including signs and symbols

- using translators, communicators and amanuenses

(b) planning, where necessary, to develop pupils' understanding through the use of all available senses and experiences by:

- using materials and resources that pupils can access through sight, touch, sound, taste or smell

- using word descriptions and other stimuli to make up for a lack of first-hand experiences

- using ICT, visual and other materials to increase pupils' knowledge of the wider world

- encouraging pupils to take part in everyday activities such as play, drama, class visits and exploring the environment

(c) planning for pupils' full participation in learning and in physical and practical activities by:

- using specialist aids and equipment

- providing support from adults or peers when needed

- adapting tasks or environments

- providing alternative activities, where necessary

(d) helping pupils to manage their behaviour, to take part in learning effectively and safely, and, at Key Stage 4, to prepare for work by:

- setting realistic demands and stating them explicitly

- using positive behaviour management, including a clear structure of rewards and sanctions

- giving pupils every chance and encouragement to develop the skills they need to work well with a partner or a group

- teaching pupils to value and respect the contribution of others

- encouraging and teaching independent working skills

- teaching essential safety rules

(e) helping individuals to manage their emotions, particularly trauma or stress, and to take part in learning by:

- identifying aspects of learning in which the pupil will engage, and planning short-term, easily achievable goals in selected activities

- providing positive feedback to reinforce and encourage learning and build self-esteem

- selecting tasks and materials sensitively to avoid unnecessary stress for the pupil

- creating a supportive learning environment in which the pupil feels safe and is able to engage with learning

- allowing time for the pupil to engage with learning, and gradually increasing the range of activities and demands

Pupils with disabilities

The QCA goes on to provide guidance on pupils with disabilities, pointing out that not all pupils with disabilities will necessarily have special educational needs, and that many learn alongside their peers with little need for additional resources beyond the aids which they use as part of their daily life, such as a wheelchair, a hearing aid or equipment to aid vision. It states that teachers' planning must ensure, however, that these pupils are enabled to participate as fully and effectively as possible in the curriculum by:

- planning appropriate amounts of time to allow for the satisfactory completion of tasks. This might involve:

  - taking account of the very slow pace at which some pupils will be able to record work, either manually or with specialist equipment, and of the physical effort required;

  - being aware of the high levels of concentration necessary for some pupils when following or interpreting text or graphics, particularly when using vision aids or tactile methods, and of the tiredness which may result;

  - allocating sufficient time, opportunity and access to equipment for pupils to gain information through experimental work and detailed observation, including the use of microscopes;

  - being aware of the effort required by some pupils to follow oral work, whether through use of residual hearing, lip reading or a signer, and of the tiredness or loss of concentration which may occur.

- planning opportunities, where necessary, for the development of skills in practical aspects of the curriculum. This might involve:

 – ensuring that all pupils can be included and participate safely in a visit to the local court as part of the citizenship course;

 – identifying aspects of Programmes of Study and attainment targets that may present specific difficulties for individuals, e.g. in PSHE/citizenship, where a more informal atmosphere may be adopted with students sitting in a circle and being encouraged to debate issues, some pupils may be uncomfortable and unsure about how to behave (particularly those with Autistic Spectrum Disorders).

Involving everyone

In Ann Ferguson and Hazel Lawson's *Access to Citizenship*, the authors reflect on how attitudes to and provision for people with learning difficulties have moved on:

> Students with learning difficulties now achieve greater levels of autonomy and independence than ever before. Instead of being considered incapable of active citizenship, they are encouraged to participate at whatever level is achievable.

> Walmsley (1991: 226) observed: 'Citizenship, as it has traditionally been conceived, has seemed an impossible status for people with learning difficulties', and commented that people with learning difficulties 'are often confined to the private world of the family' and excluded from full participation in the community. This, he suggested, was partly through lack of means to exercise their citizenship – 'lack of transport, lack of information and indeed lack of confidence to attend meetings and exercise political rights' – and partly through poverty, as many people with learning difficulties are excluded from paid work and dependent on state benefits. His observations were made more than a decade ago. In that time, citizen-advocacy and self-advocacy groups have emerged, and much ground has been covered in the move toward equality and acceptance of people with a variety of special needs.

> There is still much work to be done, however, in moving towards a more inclusive society and the PSHE/citizenship curriculum provides excellent opportunities for promoting concepts and values that positively include people with learning difficulties and disabilities.

Summary

Pupils with a wide range of needs – physical/sensory, emotional, cognitive and social – are present in increasing numbers, in all mainstream settings. Government policies point the way, with inclusion at the forefront of national policy – but it is up to teachers to make the rhetoric a reality. Teachers are ultimately responsible for all the children they teach. In terms of participation, achievement, enjoyment – the buck stops here!

CHAPTER 2

Departmental Policy

It is crucial that departmental policy describes a strategy for meeting pupils' special educational needs within the particular curricular area. There are unique challenges in this respect for the PSHE/citizenship department, in that much of the curriculum content may be delivered as part of other subjects – each with their own policies for SEN provision. In schools where citizenship and PSHE is delivered as part of tutor-group time, teachers will belong to a cross section of the various subject departments, and bringing them together to discuss policy for meeting special educational needs within that particular context may not be easy. The important thing is to ensure that this issue is not overlooked, as access to the citizenship and PSHE curriculum is vitally important to students with special needs – as well as providing valuable opportunities for all pupils to develop their awareness and understanding of individuals with 'different' behaviours and 'additional' needs. The Head of Department (who may well work in other subject areas him/herself) must be an excellent communicator and motivator who leads by example.

Any visitor to the department – from supply staff to inspectors – should be impressed by effective management when they attend a department meeting, even though some members of the department will frequently need to attend subject meetings elsewhere. The process of developing a departmental SEN policy offers the opportunity to clarify and evaluate current thinking and practice within the PSHE/citizenship team and to establish a consistent approach. One of the major strengths of the department in what may be a fairly dislocated situation is the expertise which its teachers bring to the table from other departments. No other subject department is better placed to develop learning across the curriculum.

The policy should:

- clarify the responsibilities of all staff and identify any with specialist training and/or knowledge

- describe the curriculum on offer and how it can be differentiated

- outline arrangements for assessment and reporting

- guide staff on how to work effectively with support staff

- identify staff training

The starting point will be the school's SEN policy as required by the Education Act 1996, with each subject department 'fleshing out' the detail in a way which describes how things work in practice. The writing of a policy should be much more than a paper exercise completed to satisfy the senior management team and Ofsted inspectors. As far as is humanly possible, the subject staff should come together as a team and create a framework for teaching PSHE/citizenship in a way that makes it accessible to all pupils in the school. However, the hard reality (due to teachers' commitments elsewhere in the curriculum) may be that a small number of department members may be charged with the creation and writing of policy. The meetings themselves, therefore, should focus on establishing a united approach in terms of philosophy and values.

Where to start when writing a policy

An audit can act as a starting point for reviewing current policy on SEN or can inform the writing of a new policy. It will involve gathering information and reviewing current practice with regard to pupils with SEN and is best completed by the Head of Department or a small cohort of department members, preferably with some additional advice from the SENCO. As far as possible, the audit should be carried out by the whole department, for it can provide a valuable opportunity for professional development if it is seen as an exercise in sharing good practice and encouraging joint planning. For reasons already mentioned, the audit should be timed to take place when other departments are relatively quiet (towards the end of the school year?).

However, before embarking on an audit, it is worth investing some time in a department meeting or training day, to raise awareness of special educational needs legislation and establish a shared philosophy, unless it is felt that teachers will have already gleaned this knowledge from their main subject training. Appendix 2 contains OHT layouts and an activity to use with staff. (These are also on the accompanying CD, with additional exercises you may choose to use.)

The following headings may be useful in establishing a working policy:

General statement

- What does legislation and DfES guidance say?

- What does the school policy state?

- What do members of the department have to do to comply with it?

Definition of SEN

- What does SEN mean?

- What are the areas of need and the categories used in the Code of Practice?

- Are there any special implications within the subject area?

Provision for staff within the department

- How is information shared?

- Who has responsibility for SEN within the department?

- How and when is information shared?

- Where and what information is stored?

Provision for pupils with SEN

- How are pupils with SEN assessed and monitored in the department?

- How are contributions to IEPs and reviews made?

- What criteria are used for organising teaching groups?

- What alternative courses are offered to pupils with SEN?

- What special internal and external examination arrangements are made?

- What guidance is available for working with support staff?

Resources and learning materials

- Is there any specialist equipment used in the department?

- How are resources developed?

- Where are resources stored?

Staff qualifications and Continuing Professional Development needs

- What qualifications do the members of the department have?

- What training has taken place?

- How is training planned?

- Is a record kept of training completed and training needs?

Monitoring and reviewing the policy

- How will the policy be monitored?

- When will the policy be reviewed?

The content of an SEN departmental policy

This section gives detailed information on what a SEN policy might include. Each heading is expanded with some detailed information and raises the main issues with regard to teaching pupils with SEN. At the end of each section there is an example statement. The example statements can be personalised and brought together to make a policy. All the examples in this chapter are gathered as an example policy in the appendix.

General statement with reference to the school's special educational needs policy

All schools must have an SEN policy according to the Education Act 1996. This policy will set out basic information on the school's SEN provision, and how the school identifies, assesses and provides for pupils with SEN, including information on staffing and working in partnership with other professionals and parents.

Any department policy needs to have reference to the school's SEN policy.

Example

> All members of the department will ensure that the needs of all pupils with SEN are met, according to the aims of the school and its SEN policy.

Definition of SEN

It is useful to insert at least the four areas of SEN in the department policy, as used in the Code of Practice for Special Educational Needs.

Example

TABLE 2.1 THE FOUR AREAS OF SEN

Cognition and Learning Needs	Behavioural, Emotional and Social Development Needs	Communication and Interaction Needs	Sensory and/or Physical Needs
Specific learning difficulties (SpLD)	Behavioural, emotional and social difficulties (BESD)	Speech, language and communication needs	Hearing impairment (HI)
Dyslexia	Attention Deficit Disorder (ADD)	Autistic Spectrum Disorder (ASD)	Visual impairment (VI)
Moderate learning difficulties (MLD)	Attention Deficit Hyperactivity Disorder (ADHD)	Asperger's Syndrome	Multi-sensory impairment (MSI)
Severe learning difficulties (SLD)			Physical difficulties (PD)
Profound and multiple learning difficulties (PMLD)			OTHER

Provision for staff within the department

In many schools, each department nominates a member of staff to have special responsibility for SEN provision (with or without remuneration). This can be very effective where there is a system of regular liaison between department SEN representatives and the SENCO in the form of meetings or paper communications or a mixture of both.

The responsibilities of this post may include liaison between the department and the SENCO, attending any liaison meetings and providing feedback via meetings and minutes, attending training, maintaining the departmental SEN information and records and representing the need of pupils with SEN at departmental level. This post can be seen as a valuable development opportunity for staff. The name of this person should be included in the policy.

How members of the department raise concerns about pupils with SEN can be included in this section. Concerns may be raised at specified departmental meetings before referral to the SENCO. An identified member of the department could make referrals to the SENCO and keep a record of this information.

Reference to working with support staff will include a commitment to planning and communication between staff. There may be information on inviting support staff to meetings, resources and lesson plans.

A reference to the centrally held lists of pupils with SEN and other relevant information will also be included in this section. A note about confidentiality of information should be included.

Example

> The member of staff with responsibility for overseeing the provision of SEN within the department will attend liaison meetings and feedback to other members of the department. Other responsibilities will include maintaining the department's SEN information file, attending appropriate training and disseminating this to all departmental staff. All information will be treated with confidentiality.

Provision for pupils with SEN

It is the responsibility of all staff to know which pupils have SEN and to identify any pupils having difficulties. Pupils with SEN may be identified by staff within the department in a variety of ways, these may be listed and could include:

- observation in lessons
- assessment of class work
- homework tasks
- end of module tests
- progress checks
- annual examinations
- reports

Setting out how pupils with SEN are grouped within the PSHE/citizenship department may include specifying the criteria used and/or the philosophy behind the method of grouping.

Example

> The pupils are grouped to ensure a genuine mix of ability and according to tutor information about which pupils are best taught together and which are best taught apart, and any other relevant information which may affect performance, social or medical information.
>
> Monitoring arrangements and details of how pupils can move between groups should also be set out. Information collected may include:
>
> - National Curriculum levels
> - departmental performance assessments
> - reading scores
> - advice from pastoral staff
> - discussion with staff in the SEN dept
> - information provided on IEPs

Ensuring that staff in the department understand the current legislation and guidance from central government is important, so a reference to the SEN Code of Practice and the levels of SEN intervention is helpful within the policy. Here is a good place also to put a statement about the school behaviour policy and rewards and sanctions, and how the department will make any necessary adjustments to meet the needs of pupils with SEN.

Example

It is understood that pupils with SEN may receive additional support if they have a statement of SEN, are at School Action Plus or School Action. The staff in the PSHE/citizenship department will aim to support the pupils to achieve their targets as specified on their IEPs and will provide feedback for IEP or statement reviews. Pupils with SEN will be included in the departmental monitoring system used for all pupils. Additional support will be requested as appropriate.

Resources and learning materials

The department policy needs to specify what differentiated materials are available, where they are kept and how to find new resources. This section could include a statement about working with support staff to develop resources or access specialist resources as needed, and the use of ICT. Teaching strategies may also be identified if appropriate. Advice on more specialist equipment can be sought as necessary, possibly through LEA support services: contact details may be available from the SENCO, or the department may have direct links. Any specially bought subject text or alternative/appropriate courses can be specified.

Example

The department will provide suitably differentiated materials and, where appropriate, specialist resources for pupils with SEN. Additional texts are available for those pupils working below National Curriculum level 3. Where possible, pupils with SEN will be encouraged to reach their full potential. Support staff will be provided with curriculum information in advance of lessons and will also be involved in lesson planning. A list of resources is available in the department handbook and on the noticeboard.

Staff qualifications and continuing professional development needs

It is important to recognise and record the qualifications and special skills gained by staff within the department. Training can include not only external courses but also in-house INSET and opportunities such as observing other staff, working to produce materials with other staff and visiting other establishments. Staff may have hidden skills that might enhance the work of the department and the school, for example some staff might be proficient in the use of sign language.

Where a significant element of the PSHE/citizenship curriculum is delivered through the school's tutors, it is important that the school devote some training time to whole-staff initiatives. These should be organised through the PSHE/ citizenship department, and should focus on areas of concern/development identified by them. Effectively managed, such sessions can only serve to enhance the department's standing and are likely to promote the value of what is taught to the point that teachers not involved in directly teaching the subject may want to do so in the future. It is not too much to expect schools to devote at least one full training day per year (or two half-days) to this initiative. Another worthwhile observation is that it is very important for members of senior management to attend as their absence would be a clear indication to the staff that this work is not considered important.

Example

A record of training undertaken, specialist skills and training required will be kept in the department handbook. Requests for training will be considered in line with the department and school improvement plan.

Monitoring and reviewing the policy

To be effective, any policy needs regular monitoring and review. These can be planned as part of the yearly cycle. The responsibility for the monitoring can rest with the Head of Department, but will have more effect if supported by someone from outside acting as a critical friend. This could be the SENCO or a member of the senior management team in school.

Example

The department SEN policy will be monitored by the Head of Department on a planned annual basis, with advice being sought from the SENCO as part of a three-yearly review process.

Conclusion

Creating a departmental SEN policy should be a developmental activity to improve the teaching and learning for all pupils but especially for those with special or additional needs. The policy should be a working document that will evolve and change; it is there to challenge current practice and to encourage improvement for both pupils and staff. If departmental staff work together to create the policy, they will have ownership of it; it will have true meaning and be effective in clarifying practice.

CHAPTER 3

Different Types of SEN

This chapter is a starting point for information on the special educational needs most frequently occurring in the mainstream secondary school. It describes the main characteristics of each learning difficulty with practical ideas for use in subject areas, and contacts for further information. Some of the tips are based on good secondary practice while others encourage teachers to try new or less familiar approaches.

The special educational needs outlined in this chapter are grouped under the headings used in the SEN Code of Practice (DfES 2001):

- cognition and learning

- behavioural, emotional and social development

- communication and interaction

- sensory and/or physical needs

(See Table 2.1 in Chapter 2.)

The labels used in this chapter are useful when describing pupils' difficulties, but it is important to remember not to use the label in order to define the pupil. Put the pupil before the difficulty, saying 'the pupil with special educational needs' rather than 'the SEN pupil', 'pupils with MLD' rather than 'MLDs'.

Remember to take care in using labels when talking with parents, pupils or other professionals. Unless a pupil has a firm diagnosis, and parents and pupil understand the implications of that diagnosis, it is more appropriate to describe the features of the special educational need rather than use the label, for example a teacher might describe a pupil's spelling difficulties but not use the term 'dyslexic'.

The number and profile of pupils with special educational needs will vary from school to school, so it is important to consider the pupil with SEN as an individual within your school and subject environment. The strategies contained in this chapter will help teachers adapt that environment to meet the needs of individual pupils within the subject context. For example, rather than saying, 'He can't read the worksheet', recognise that the worksheet is too difficult for the pupil, and adapt the work accordingly.

There is a continuum of need within each of the special educational needs listed here. Some pupils will be affected more than others, and show fewer or more of the characteristics described.

The availability and levels of support from professionals within a school (e.g. SENCOs, support teachers, Teaching Assistants) and external professionals (e.g. educational psychologists, Learning Support Service staff, medical staff) will depend on the severity of pupils' SEN. This continuum of need will also impact on the subject teacher's planning and allocation of support staff.

Pupils with other less common special educational needs may be included in some secondary schools, and additional information on these conditions may be found in a variety of sources. These include the school SENCO, LEA support services, educational psychologists and the Internet.

Asperger's Syndrome

Asperger's Syndrome is a disorder at the able end of the autistic spectrum. People with Asperger's Syndrome have average to high intelligence but share the same Triad of Impairments. They often want to make friends but do not understand the complex rules of social interaction. They have impaired fine and gross motor skills, with writing being a particular problem. Boys are more likely to be affected – with the ratio being 10:1 boys to girls. Because they appear 'odd' and naïve, these pupils are particularly vulnerable to bullying.

Main characteristics:

- **Social interaction**

  Pupils with Asperger's Syndrome want friends but have not developed the strategies necessary for making and sustaining friendships. They find it very difficult to learn social norms and to pick up on social cues. Highly social situations, such as lessons, can cause great anxiety.

- **Social communication**

  Pupils have appropriate spoken language but tend to sound formal and pedantic, using little expression and with an unusual tone of voice. They have difficulty using and understanding non-verbal language, such as facial expression, gesture, body language and eye-contact. They have a literal understanding of language and do not grasp implied meanings.

- **Social imagination**

  Pupils with Asperger's Syndrome need structured environments, and routines they understand and can anticipate. They excel at learning facts and figures, but have difficulty understanding abstract concepts and generalising information and skills. They often have all-consuming special interests.

How can the subject teacher help?

- Liaise closely with parents, especially over homework.
- Create as calm a classroom environment as possible.
- Allow the pupil to sit in the same place for each lesson.
- Set up a work buddy system for your lessons.
- Provide additional visual cues in class.
- Give time for the pupil to process questions and respond.
- Make sure pupils understand what to do.
- Allow alternatives to writing for recording.
- Use visual timetables and task activity lists.
- Prepare for changes to routines well in advance.
- Give written homework instructions and stick them into an exercise book.
- Have your own class rules and apply them consistently.

The National Autistic Society, 393 City Road, London EC1V 1NG
Tel: 0845 070 4004 Helpline (10a.m.–4p.m., Mon–Fri) Tel: 020 7833 2299
Fax: 020 7833 9666
Email: nas@nas.org.uk   Website: http://www.nas.org.uk

Attention Deficit Disorder (with or without hyperactivity) (ADD/ADHD)

Attention Deficit Hyperactivity Disorder is a term used to describe children who exhibit over-active behaviour and impulsivity and who have difficulty in paying attention. It is caused by a form of brain dysfunction of a genetic nature. ADHD can sometimes be controlled effectively by medication. Children of all levels of ability can have ADHD.

Main characteristics:

- difficulty in following instructions and completing tasks
- easily distracted by noise, movement of others, objects attracting attention
- often doesn't listen when spoken to
- fidgets and becomes restless, can't sit still
- interferes with other pupils' work
- can't stop talking, interrupts others, calls out
- runs about when inappropriate
- has difficulty in waiting or taking turns
- acts impulsively without thinking about the consequences

How can the subject teacher help?

- Make eye contact and use the pupil's name when speaking to him.
- Keep instructions simple – the one sentence rule.
- Provide clear routines and rules, and rehearse them regularly.
- Sit the pupil away from obvious distractions, e.g. windows, the computer.
- In busy situations direct the pupil by name to visual or practical objects.
- Encourage the pupil to repeat back instructions before starting work.
- Tell the pupil when to begin a task.
- Give two choices – avoid the option of the pupil saying 'No': 'Do you want to write in blue or black pen?'
- Give advanced warning when something is about to happen, change or finish with a time, e.g. 'In two minutes I need you (pupil name) to ...'
- Give specific praise – catch him being good, give attention for positive behaviour.
- Give the pupil responsibilities so that others can see him/her in a positive light and he develops a positive self-image.

ADD Information Services, PO Box 340, Edgware, Middlesex, HA8 9HL
Tel: 020 8906 9068
ADDNET UK www.btinternet.com/~black.ice/addnet/

Autistic Spectrum Disorders (ASD)

The term 'Autistic Spectrum Disorders' is used for a range of disorders affecting the development of social interaction, social communication and social imagination and flexibility of thought. This is known as the 'Triad of Impairments'. Pupils with ASD cover the full range of ability, and the severity of the impairment varies widely. Some pupils also have learning disabilities or other difficulties. Four times as many boys as girls are diagnosed with an ASD.

Main characteristics:

- **Social interaction**
  Pupils with an ASD find it difficult to understand social behaviour and this affects their ability to interact with children and adults. They do not always understand social contexts. They may experience high levels of stress and anxiety in settings that do not meet their needs or when routines are changed. This can lead to inappropriate behaviour.

- **Social communication**
  Understanding and use of non-verbal and verbal communication is impaired. Pupils with an ASD have difficulty understanding the communication of others and in developing effective communication themselves. They have a literal understanding of language. Many are delayed in learning to speak, and some never develop speech at all.

- **Social imagination and flexibility of thought**
  Pupils with an ASD have difficulty in thinking and behaving flexibly which may result in restricted, obsessional or repetitive activities. They are often more interested in objects than people, and have intense interests in one particular area such as trains and vacuum cleaners. Pupils work best when they have a routine. Unexpected changes in those routines will cause distress. Some pupils with Autistic Spectrum Disorders have a different perception of sounds, sights, smell, touch and taste, and this can affect their response to these sensations.

How can the subject teacher help?

- Liaise with parents as they will have many useful strategies.
- Provide visual supports in class: objects, pictures, etc.
- Give a symbolic or written timetable for each day.
- Give advance warning of any changes to usual routines.
- Provide either an individual desk or with a work buddy.
- Avoid using too much eye contact as it can cause distress.
- Give individual instructions using the pupil's name, e.g. 'Paul, bring me your book'.
- Allow access to computers.
- Develop social interactions using a buddy system or Circle of Friends.
- Avoid using metaphor, idiom or sarcasm –say what you mean in simple language.
- Use special interests to motivate.
- Allow difficult situations to be rehearsed by means of Social Stories.

BEHAVIOURAL, EMOTIONAL AND SOCIAL DEVELOPMENT NEEDS

This term includes behavioural, emotional and social difficulties and Attention Deficit Disorder with or without hyperactivity. These difficulties can be seen across the whole ability range and have a continuum of severity. Pupils with special educational needs in this category are those that have persistent difficulties despite an effective school behaviour policy and a personal and social curriculum.

(See p. 23 for notes on Attention Deficit Disorder.)

Behavioural, emotional and social difficulty (BESD)

Main characteristics:

- inattentive, poor concentration and lack of interest in school/school work
- easily frustrated, anxious about changes
- unable to work in groups
- unable to work independently, constantly seeking help
- confrontational – verbally aggressive towards pupils and/or adults
- physically aggressive towards pupils and/or adults
- destroys property – their own/others
- appears withdrawn, distressed, unhappy, sulky, may self-harm
- lacks confidence, acts extremely frightened, lacks self-esteem
- finds it difficult to communicate
- finds it difficult to accept praise

How can the subject teacher help?

- Check the ability level of the pupil and adapt the level of work to this.
- Consider the pupil's strengths and use them.
- Tell the pupil what you expect in advance, as regards work and behaviour.
- Talk to the pupil to find out a bit about them.
- Set a subject target with a reward system.
- Focus your comments on the behaviour not on the pupil and offer an alternative way of behaving when correcting the pupil.
- Use positive language and verbal praise whenever possible.
- Tell the pupil what you want them to do: 'I need you to ...', 'I want you to ...', rather than ask. This avoids confrontation and allows the possibility that there is room for negotiation.
- Give the pupil a choice between two options.
- Stick to what you say.
- Involve the pupil in responsibilities to increase self-esteem and confidence.
- Plan a 'time out' system. Ask a colleague for help with this.

SEBDA is the new name for the Association of Workers for Children with emotional and behavioural difficulties.
www.awcebd.co.uk

Cerebral palsy (CP)

Cerebral palsy is a persistent disorder of movement and posture. It is caused by damage or lack of development to part of the brain before or during birth or in early childhood. Problems vary from slight clumsiness to more severe lack of control of movements. Pupils with CP may also have learning difficulties. They may use a wheelchair or other mobility aid.

Main characteristics:

There are three main forms of cerebral palsy:

- *spasticity* – disordered control of movement associated with stiffened muscles

- *athetosis* – frequent involuntary movements

- *ataxia* – an unsteady gait with balance difficulties and poor spatial awareness

  Pupils may also have communication difficulties.

How can the subject teacher help?

- Talk to parents, the physiotherapist – and the pupil.

- Consider the classroom layout.

- Have high academic expectations.

- Use visual supports: objects, pictures, symbols.

- Arrange a work/subject buddy.

- Speak directly to the pupil rather than through a Teaching Assistant.

- Ensure access to appropriate IT equipment for the subject – and that it is used.

Scope, PO Box 833, Milton Keynes, MK12 5NY
Tel: 0808 800 3333 (Freephone helpline) Fax: 01908 321051
Email: cphelpline@scope.org.uk   Website: http://www.scope.org.uk

---

Down's Syndrome (DS)

Down's Syndrome is the most common identifiable cause of learning disability. This is a genetic condition caused by the presence of an extra chromosome 21. People with DS have varying degrees of learning difficulties ranging from mild to severe. They have a specific learning profile with characteristic strengths and weaknesses. All share certain physical characteristics but will also inherit family traits in physical features and personality. They may have additional sight, hearing, respiratory, and heart problems.

Main characteristics:

- delayed motor skills
- take longer to learn and consolidate new skills
- limited concentration
- difficulties with generalisation, thinking and reasoning
- sequencing difficulties
- stronger visual than aural skills
- better social than academic skills

How can the subject teacher help?

- Sit the pupil in the best position to see and hear.
- Speak directly to the pupil and reinforce with facial expression, pictures and objects.
- Use simple, familiar language in short sentences.
- Check instructions have been understood.
- Give time for the pupil to process information and formulate a response.
- Break lessons up into a series of shorter, varied, and achievable tasks.
- Accept other ways of recording: drawings, tape/video recordings, symbols, etc.
- Set differentiated tasks linked to the work of the rest of the class.
- Provide age-appropriate resources and activities.
- Allow working in top sets to give good behaviour models.
- Provide a work buddy.
- Expect unsupported work for part of each lesson.

The Downs Association, 155 Mitcham Road, London SW17 9PG
Tel: 0845 230 0372
Email: info@downs-syndrome.org.uk
Website: http://www.downs-syndrome.org.uk

Fragile X Syndrome

Fragile X Syndrome is caused by a malformation of the X chromosome and is the most common form of inherited learning disability. This intellectual disability varies widely, with up to a third having learning problems ranging from moderate to severe. More boys than girls are affected but both may be carriers.

Main characteristics:

- delayed and disordered speech and language development

- difficulties with the social use of language

- articulation and/or fluency difficulties

- verbal skills better developed than reasoning skills

- repetitive or obsessive behaviour, such as hand-flapping, chewing, etc.

- clumsiness and fine motor co-ordination problems

- attention deficit and hyperactivity

- easily anxious or overwhelmed in busy environments

How can the subject teacher help?

- Liaise with parents.

- Make sure the pupil knows what is to happen in each lesson – provide visual timetables, work schedules or written lists.

- Ensure the pupil sits at the front of the class, in the same seat for all lessons.

- Arrange a work/subject buddy.

- Where possible keep to routines and give prior warning of all changes.

- Make instructions clear and simple.

- Use visual supports: objects, pictures, symbols.

- Allow the pupil to use a computer to record and access information.

- Give lots of praise and positive feedback.

Fragile X Society, Rood End House, 6 Stortford Road, Dunmow, CM6 1DA
Tel: 01424 813147 (Helpline) Tel: 01371 875100 (Office)
Email: info@fragilex.org.uk   Website: http://www.fragilex.org.uk

Moderate learning difficulties (MLD)

The term 'moderate learning difficulties' is used to describe pupils who find it extremely difficult to achieve expected levels of attainment across the curriculum, even with a differentiated and flexible approach. These pupils do not find learning easy and can suffer from low self-esteem and sometime exhibit unacceptable behaviour as a way of avoiding failure.

Main characteristics

- difficulties with reading, writing and comprehension
- unable to understand and retain basic mathematical skills and concepts
- immature social and emotional skills
- limited vocabulary and communication skills
- short attention span
- under-developed co-ordination skills
- lack of logical reasoning
- inability to transfer and apply skills to different situations
- have difficulty remembering what has been taught
- difficulty with organising themselves, following a timetable, remembering books and equipment

How can the subject teacher help?

- Check the pupil's strengths, weaknesses and attainment levels.
- Establish a routine within the lesson.
- Keep tasks short and varied.
- Keep listening tasks short or broken up with activities.
- Provide word lists, writing frames, shorten text.
- Try alternative methods of recording information, e.g. drawings, charts, labelling, diagrams, use of ICT.
- Check previously gained knowledge and build on this.
- Repeat information in different ways.
- Show the child what to do or what the expected outcome is, demonstrate or show examples of completed work.
- Use practical, concrete, visual examples to illustrate explanations.
- Question the pupil to check they have grasped a concept or can follow instructions.
- Make sure the pupil always has something to do.
- Use lots of praise, instant rewards – catch them trying hard.

The MLD Alliance, c/o The Elfrida Society, 34 Islington Park Street, London N1 1PX
www.mldalliance.com/excutive.htm

Physical disability (PD)

There is a wide range of physical disabilities, and pupils with PD cover all academic abilities. Some pupils are able to access the curriculum and learn effectively without additional educational provision. They have a disability but do not have a special educational need. For other pupils, the impact on their education may be severe, and the school will need to make adjustments to enable them to access the curriculum.

Some pupils with a physical disability have associated medical conditions which may impact on their mobility. These include cerebral palsy, heart disease, spina bifida and hydrocephalus, and muscular dystrophy. Pupils with physical disabilities may also have sensory impairments, neurological problems or learning difficulties. They may use a wheelchair and/or additional mobility aids. Some pupils will be mobile but may have significant fine motor difficulties that require support. Others may need augmentative or alternative communication aids.

Pupils with a physical disability may need to miss lessons to attend physiotherapy or medical appointments. They are also likely to become very tired as they expend greater effort to complete everyday tasks. Schools will need to be flexible and sensitive to individual pupil needs.

How can the subject teacher help?

- Get to know pupils and parents and they will help you make the right adjustments.

- Maintain high expectations.

- Consider the classroom layout.

- Allow the pupil to leave lessons a few minutes early to avoid busy corridors and give time to get to next lesson.

- Set homework earlier in the lesson so instructions are not missed.

- Speak directly to pupil rather than through a Teaching Assistant.

- Let pupils make their own decisions.

- Ensure access to appropriate IT equipment for the lesson – and that it is used!

- Give alternative ways of recording work.

- Plan to cover work missed through medical or physiotherapy appointments.

- Be sensitive to fatigue, especially at the end of the school day.

Semantic Pragmatic Disorder (SPD)

Semantic Pragmatic Disorder is a communication disorder which falls within the autistic spectrum. 'Semantic' refers to the meanings of words and phrases and 'pragmatic' refers to the use of language in a social context. Pupils with this disorder have difficulties understanding the meaning of what people say and in using language to communicate effectively. Pupils with SPD find it difficult to extract the central meaning – saliency – of situations.

Main characteristics:

- delayed language development

- fluent speech but may sound stilted or over-formal

- may repeat phrases out of context from videos or adult conversations

- difficulty understanding abstract concepts

- limited or inappropriate use of eye contact, facial expression or gesture

- motor skills problems

How can the subject teacher help?

- Sit the pupil at the front of the room to avoid distractions.

- Use visual supports: objects, pictures, symbols.

- Pair with a work/subject buddy.

- Create a calm working environment with clear classroom rules.

- Be specific and unambiguous when giving instructions.

- Make sure instructions are understood, especially when using subject-specific vocabulary that can have another meaning in a different context.

AFASIC, 2nd Floor, 50–52 Great Sutton Street, London EC1V 0DJ
Tel: 0845 355 5577 (Helpline 11a.m.–2p.m.) Tel: 020 7490 9410 Fax: 020 7251 2834
Email: info@afasic.org.uk   Website: http://www.afasic.org.uk

Sensory impairments

Hearing impairment (HI)

The term 'hearing impairment' is a generic term used to describe all hearing loss. The main types of loss are monaural, conductive, sensory and mixed loss. The degree of hearing loss is described as mild, moderate, severe or profound. Some children rely on lip reading, others will use hearing aids, and a small proportion will have British Sign Language (BSL) as their primary means of communication.

How can the subject teacher help?

- Check the degree of loss the pupil has.

- Check the best seating position (e.g. away from the hum of OHP, computers, with good ear to speaker).

- Check that the pupil can see your face for facial expressions and lip reading.

- Provide a list of vocabulary, context and visual clues, especially for new subjects.

- During class discussion allow only one pupil to speak at a time and indicate where the speaker is.

- Check that any aids are working and if there is any other specialist equipment available.

- Make sure the light falls on your face and lips. Do not stand with your back to a window.

- If you use interactive whiteboards, ensure that the beam does not prevent the pupil from seeing your face.

- Ban small talk.

Royal Institute for the Deaf (RNID), 19–23 Featherstone Street, London EC1Y 8SL
Tel: 0808 808 0123
British Deaf Association (BDA) 1–3 Worship Street, London EC2A 2AB
British Association of Teachers of the Deaf (BATOD), The Orchard, Leven, North Humberside HU17 5QA

Visual impairment (VI)

Visual impairment refers to a range of difficulties, including those experienced by pupils with monocular vision (vision in one eye), those who are partially sighted and those who are blind. Pupils with visual impairment cover the whole ability range and some pupils may have other SEN.

How can the subject teacher help?

- Find out the degree of visual impairment.

- Check the optimum position for the pupil, e.g. for a monocular pupil their good eye should be towards the action.

- Always provide the pupil with his own copy of the text.

- Provide enlarged print copies of written text.

- Check use of ICT (enlarged icons, talking text, teach keyboard skills).

- Do not stand with your back to the window as this creates a silhouette and makes it harder for the pupil to see you.

- Draw the pupil's attention to displays – which they may not notice.

- Make sure the floor is kept free of clutter.

- Tell the pupil if there is a change to the layout of a space.

- Ask if there is any specialist equipment available (enlarged print dictionaries, lights, talking scales).

Royal National Institute for the Blind (RNIB), 224, Great Portland St, London W1W 5AA
Tel: 020 7388 1266
Website: www.mid.org.uk

Multi-sensory impairment

Pupils with multi-sensory impairment have a combination of visual and hearing difficulties. They may also have other additional disabilities that make their situation complex. A pupil with these difficulties is likely to have a high level of individual support.

How can the subject teacher help?

- The subject teacher will need to liaise with support staff to ascertain the appropriate provision within each subject.

- Consideration will need to be given to alternative means of communication.

- Be prepared to be flexible and to adapt tasks, targets and assessment procedures.

Severe learning difficulties (SLD)

This term covers a wide and varied group of pupils who have significant intellectual or cognitive impairments. Many have communication difficulties and/or sensory impairments in addition to more general cognitive impairments. They may also have difficulties in mobility, co-ordination and perception. Some pupils may use signs and symbols to support their communication and understanding. Their attainments may be within or below level 1 of the National Curriculum, or in the upper P scale range (P4–P8), for much of their school careers.

How can the subject teacher help?

- Liaise with parents.

- Arrange a work/subject buddy.

- Use visual supports: objects, pictures, symbols.

- Learn some signs relevant to the subject.

- Allow time to process information and formulate responses.

- Set differentiated tasks linked to the work of the rest of the class.

- Set achievable targets for each lesson or module of work.

- Accept different recording methods: drawings, audio or video recordings, photographs, etc.

- Give access to computers where appropriate.

- Give a series of short, varied activities within each lesson.

Profound and multiple learning difficulties (PMLD)

Pupils with profound and multiple learning difficulties (PMLD) have complex learning needs. In addition to very severe learning difficulties, pupils have other significant difficulties, such as physical disabilities, sensory impairments or severe medical conditions. Pupils with PMLD require a high level of adult support, both for their learning needs and for their personal care.

They are able to access the curriculum through sensory experiences and stimulation. Some pupils communicate by gesture, eye pointing or symbols, others by very simple language. Their attainments are likely to remain in the early P scale range (P1–P4) throughout their school careers (that is below level 1 of the National Curriculum). The P scales provide small, achievable steps to monitor progress. Some pupils will make no progress or may even regress because of associated medical conditions. For this group, experiences are as important as attainment.

How can the subject teacher help?

- Liaise with parents and Teaching Assistants.

- Consider the classroom layout.

- Identify possible sensory experiences in your lessons.

- Use additional sensory supports: objects, pictures, fragrances, music, movements, food, etc.

- Take photographs to record experiences and responses.

- Set up a work/subject buddy rota for the class.

- Identify times when the pupil can work with groups.

MENCAP, 117–123 Golden Lane, London EC1Y 0RT
Tel: 020 7454 0454 Website: http://www.mencap.org.uk

SPECIFIC LEARNING DIFFICULTIES (SpLD)

The term 'specific learning difficulties' covers dyslexia, dyscalculia and dyspraxia.

Dyslexia

The term 'dyslexia' is used to describe a learning difficulty associated with words and it can affect a pupil's ability to read, write and/or spell. Research has shown that there is no one definitive definition of dyslexia or one identified cause, and it has a wide range of symptoms. Although found across a whole range of ability levels, the idea that dyslexia presents as a difficulty between expected outcomes and performance is widely held.

Main characteristics

- The pupil may frequently lose their place while reading, make a lot of errors with the high frequency words, have difficulty reading names and have difficulty blending sounds and segmenting words. Reading requires a great deal of effort and concentration.

- The pupil's written work may seem messy with crossing outs, similarly shaped letters may be confused, such as b/d/p/q, m/w, n/u, and letters in words may be jumbled, such as tired/tried. Spelling difficulties often persist into adult life and these pupils become reluctant writers.

How can the subject teacher help?

- Be aware of the type of difficulty and the pupil's strengths.

- Teach and allow the use of word processing, spell checkers and computer-aided learning packages.

- Provide word lists and photocopies of copying from the board.

- Consider alternative recording methods, e.g. pictures, plans, flow charts, mind maps.

- Allow extra time for tasks, including assessments and examinations.

Dyscalculia

The term 'dyscalculia' is used to describe a difficulty in mathematics. This might be either a marked discrepancy between the pupil's developmental level and general ability on measures of specific maths ability, or a total inability to abstract or consider concepts and numbers.

Main characteristics:

- *In number*, the pupil may have difficulty counting by rote, writing or reading numbers, miss out or reverse numbers, have difficulty with mental maths, and be unable to remember concepts, rules and formulae.

- *In maths based concepts*, the pupil may have difficulty with money, telling the time, with directions, right and left, with sequencing events or may lose track of turns, e.g. in team games, dance.

How can the subject teacher help?

- Provide number/word/rule/formulae lists and photocopies of copying from the board.

- Make use of ICT and teach the use of calculators.

- Encourage the use of rough paper for working out.

- Plan the setting out of work with it well spaced on the page.

- Provide practical objects that are age appropriate to aid learning.

- Allow extra time for tasks, including assessments and examinations.

Dyspraxia

The term 'dyspraxia' is used to describe an immaturity with the way in which the brain processes information, resulting in messages not being properly transmitted.

Main characteristics:

- difficulty in co-ordinating movements, may appear awkward and clumsy

- difficulty with handwriting and drawing, throwing and catching

- difficulty following sequential events, e.g. multiple instructions

- may misinterpret situations, take things literally which results in frustration and irritability

- limited social skills and become frustrated and irritable

- some articulation difficulties (see verbal dyspraxia)

How can the subject teacher help?

- Be sensitive to the pupil's limitations in games and outdoor activities and plan tasks to enable success.

- Ask the pupil questions to check his/her understanding of instructions/tasks.

- Check seating position to encourage good presentation (both feet resting on the floor, desk at elbow height and ideally with a sloping surface to work on).

www.dyscalculia.co.uk
The British Dyslexia Association
Tel: 0118 966 8271 www.bda-dyslexia.org.uk
Dyslexia Institute
Tel: 07184 222 300 www.dyslexia-inst.org.uk

Speech, Language and Communication Difficulties (SLCD)

Pupils with speech, language and communication difficulties have problems understanding what others say and/or making others understand what they say. Their development of speech and language skills may be significantly delayed. Speech and language difficulties are very common in young children but most problems are resolved during the primary years. Problems that persist beyond the transfer to secondary school will be more severe. Any problem affecting speech, language and communication will have a significant effect on a pupil's self-esteem, and personal and social relationships. The development of literacy skills is also likely to be affected. Even where pupils learn to decode, they may not understand what they have read. Sign language gives pupils an additional method of communication. Pupils with speech, language and communication difficulties cover the whole range of academic abilities.

Main characteristics:

- **Speech difficulties**
  Pupils who have difficulties with expressive language may experience problems in articulation and the production of speech sounds, or in co-ordinating the muscles that control speech. They may have a stammer or some other form of dysfluency.

- **Language/communication difficulties**
  Pupils with receptive language impairments have difficulty understanding the meaning of what others say. They may use words incorrectly with inappropriate grammatical patterns, have a reduced vocabulary, or find it hard to recall words and express ideas. Some pupils will also have difficulty using and understanding eye-contact, facial expression, gesture and body language.

How can the subject teacher help?

- Talk to parents, speech therapist – and the pupil.
- Learn the most common signs for your subject.
- Use visual supports: objects, pictures, symbols.
- Use the pupil's name when addressing them.
- Give one instruction at a time, using short, simple sentences.
- Give time to respond before repeating a question.
- Make sure pupils understand what they have to do before starting a task.
- Pair with a work/subject buddy.
- Give access to a computer or other IT equipment appropriate to the subject.
- Give written homework instructions.

ICAN 4 Dyer's Buildings, Holborn, London EC1N 2QP
Tel: 0845 225 4071
Email: info@ican.org.uk   website: http://www.ican.org.uk
AFASIC 2nd Floor, 50–52 Great Sutton Street, London EC1V 0DJ
Tel: 0845 355 5577 (Helpline) Tel: 020 7490 9410   Fax 020 7251 2834
Email: info@afasic.org.uk   Website: http://www.afasic.org.uk

Tourette's Syndrome (TS)

Tourette's Syndrome is a neurological disorder characterised by tics. Tics are involuntary, rapid or sudden movements or sounds that are frequently repeated. There is a wide range of severity of the condition with some people having no need to seek medical help while others have a socially disabling condition. The tics can be suppressed for a short time but will be more noticeable when the pupil is anxious or excited.

Main characteristics:

Physical tics
These range from simple blinking or nodding, through more complex movements, to more extreme conditions such as echopraxia (imitating actions seen) or copropraxia (repeatedly making obscene gestures).

Vocal tics
Vocal tics may be as simple as throat clearing or coughing, but can progress to be as extreme as echolalia (the repetition of what was last heard) or coprolalia (the repetition of obscene words).

TS itself causes no behavioural or educational problems but other, associated, disorders such as Attention Deficit Hyperactivity Disorder (ADHD) or Obsessive Compulsive Disorder (OCD) may be present.

How can the subject teacher help?

- Establish a rapport with the pupil.

- Talk to the parents.

- Agree an 'escape route' signal should the tics become disruptive.

- Allow pupil to sit at the back of the room to prevent staring.

- Give access to a computer to reduce handwriting.

- Make sure pupil is not teased or bullied.

- Be alert for signs of anxiety or depression.

Tourette Syndrome (UK) Association
PO Box 26149, Dunfermline, KY12 7YU
Tel: 0845 458 1252 (Helpline) Tel: 01383 629600 (Admin.) Fax: 01383 629609
Email: enquiries@tsa.org.uk   Website: http://www.tsa.org.uk

See Appendix 3 for an INSET activity designed to familiarise staff with the characteristics of various SEN and with appropriate strategies.

CHAPTER 4

The Inclusive Citizenship Classroom

Why PSHE and citizenship are particularly suited to inclusive education

If we may style personal, social and health education (PSHE) and citizenship as two discrete subjects within the secondary curriculum, then it is hard to think of two subjects more closely set at the heart of inclusive education. To take PSHE first of all, the DfES sets out a series of non-statutory guidelines which govern what a pupil should be taught. It is well worth the reading time of any PSHE teacher to go through these guidelines in full, but merely examining the heading under which each set of guidelines is arranged speaks volumes:

- Developing confidence and responsibility and making the most of [pupils'] abilities

- Developing a healthy, safer lifestyle

- Developing good relationships and respecting the difference between people

Under this last heading, for example, pupils are to be taught 'about the effects of all types of stereotyping ... and discrimination and how to challenge them assertively'. Pupils are also to be taught empathy with people different from themselves, as well as the nature of friendship and how to make and keep friends and, the crowning guideline: 'to communicate confidently with their peers and adults'.

Moving on to examine the 'breadth of opportunities' which should be available to pupils at Key Stage 3 in PSHE, the guidelines recommend that pupils be taught the knowledge, skills and understanding through opportunities to take responsibility, feel positive about themselves, participate, make real choices and decisions, meet and work with people, develop relationships, consider social and moral dilemmas, find information and advice and prepare for change. In itself, it could be argued that this represents a syllabus for inclusive education!

As pupils move up from Key Stage 3 to Key Stage 4, their ability to take greater responsibility for 'acts of citizenship' within the school and the wider community become apparent. The committed PSHE teacher is looking for this change within the individual rather than for a beautifully maintained exercise book.

> Have there been occasions within your experience of teaching PSHE when it was important to achieve a finished product?

An important difference between PSHE and citizenship

There is a very important difference between the status of the guidelines for citizenship and those for PSHE, and that is concerned with their statutory nature. All good schools teach both PSHE and citizenship, of course, but citizenship *must* be taught, so its guidelines are statutory and were made so by Act of Parliament in 1998. It is worth reflecting on some of the quotations which are used to introduce citizenship in *The National Curriculum Handbook*:

> - 'Create a society where people matter more than things.' (Archbishop Desmond Tutu)
> - 'It is only when you know how to be a citizen of your own country that you can learn how to be a citizen of the world.' (Terry Waite CBE)
> - 'We need to be aware of the [racial] diversity that exists in our society and value each individual.' (Doreen Lawrence)

All three of these quotations could serve as beacons to promote inclusion in schools, as well as citizenship.

Citizenship, taught well, can impart to young people some of the tools required for action in their adult life. Knowing about legal and human rights and associated responsibilities, along with how our criminal and civic justice systems work, represents a 'skill area' which all young people will need.

Similarly, in learning about our national diversity, how ironic it would be if we did not give *all* our pupils the opportunity to participate.

In all, there are nine strands of knowledge and understanding, with four vital themes, about which all young people should learn, and preferably learn together:

- voting

- resolving conflict fairly

- understanding the significance of the media

- developing a notion of global interdependence and responsibility

By learning together, without exclusion, the classroom is reflecting more truly the values that are being taught.

> Is teaching pupils their rights meaningful if these rights are likely to be interpreted to them by other responsible adults throughout their lives?

Some challenges inherent in an inclusive approach to PSHE and citizenship

In considering the 'Developing skills of participation and responsible action' section of the citizenship curriculum, however, we can better appreciate the difficulties encountered when teaching citizenship to inclusive groups:

The guidelines state that pupils should be taught to:

(a) use their imagination to consider other people's experiences and be able to think about, express, explain and critically evaluate views that are not their own;

(b) negotiate, decide and take part responsibly in school and community-based activities;

(c) reflect on the process of participating.

Pause to consider the verbs that are used in this instruction: 'use imagination', 'consider', 'express', 'explain', 'critically evaluate', 'negotiate', 'decide', 'take part responsibly', 'reflect'.

The emphasis in these verbs is on the abstract (as opposed to verbs such as paint, read, walk, run, etc. which emphasise the concrete). In highlighting this feature of the citizenship curriculum (which is, of course, also present in many aspects of PSHE and other areas of the curriculum), we have focused upon an important issue to be addressed when trying to make our teaching more inclusive. The accent needs to be on active learning which is contextual and incorporates appropriate 'concrete' experiences and examples if pupils with SEN are to make good progress.

Being overly concerned with reading, writing and non-co-operative learning will put up significant barriers to making inclusion work. PSHE and citizenship teachers ought not to become obsessed with the quantity of work 'done' (which all too often refers to the amount of writing) as opposed to the quality of classroom interaction. In an inclusive PSHE/citizenship environment, the delineation between teacher and taught will sometimes be less clear, as there will be occasions when peer tutoring is appropriate. Similarly, paired and group work will be a frequent feature of active teaching.

Because teachers often feel exam and curriculum-driven, they can become nervous and lacking in confidence when they are advised to actually take their metaphorical foot 'off the accelerator'. Perhaps, therefore, it is worth considering the four ways in which citizenship is expected to contribute to the Key Stage 3 National Strategy:

- *Raising expectations* – encourages all pupils to make informed choices about teaching and learning opportunities, reflect on achievements and plan future learning targets.

- *Ensuring progression* – provides a context for induction into new school communities and builds upon Key Stage 2 citizenship experiences.

- *Engaging and motivating* – is relevant to pupils' interests and needs, thus encouraging them to think critically and enquire about topical issues, problems and events.

- *Transforming teaching and learning* – requires a range of active, participatory teaching and learning approaches, and work within communities beyond the school.

Emphasising that citizenship is an entitlement for *all* pupils, QCA documentation points out the three principles for inclusion within the subject:

- setting suitable learning challenges;

- responding to pupils' diverse learning needs;

- overcoming potential barriers to learning and assessment for individuals and groups of pupils.

Within inclusive learning environments and effective PSHE and citizenship education, six characteristics are apparent:

- the contributions of all are valued;

- all feel secure and able to continue;

- stereotypical views are challenged;

- diversity is appreciated;

- individuals take responsibility for their actions;

- bullying and harrassment are challenged.

All of the principles and characteristics outlined above are laudable: the central task of this resource is to consider how we put them into action.

> Is it possible to identify those areas of the citizenship curriculum which will prove most challenging to pupils with learning difficulties?

Realistic demands in terms of language and understanding

PSHE and citizenship are 'subjects' which are very concept-driven. No narrow, academic syllabus would suffice since they are concerned with the actual process of living life. It would be useful, therefore at this point, to examine the requirements in terms of language and understanding which it would be reasonable to expect of pupils. Initially, when pupils are introduced to the idea of active citizenship, they should be introduced to the notion of rights as well as responsibilities, and how the two are mutually dependent. Rather than dwelling on these concepts in the abstract, the PSHE/citizenship teacher can make a positive connection between these and rules at home and in their school communities.

The teacher could, for example, point out to the class that people have the right to own a dog, but would have that dog taken away from them by a court if they did not show responsibility. The teacher could then ask pupils to whom the responsibility is owed until, with teacher guidance, they have arrived at the notions of responsibility to the community and to the dog itself.

Pupils could be asked to think of *four* responsibilities dog owners have towards their charge (proper feeding, exercise, shelter and comfort, reasonable toilet arrangments). Then pupils could think of four responsibilities dog owners have to the community in which the dog lives (not allowing the dog to run wild, giving the dog basic obedience training, ensuring it does not attack other people or dogs and cleaning up after its toilet). An activity sheet for this topic is provided in Appendix 4.1.

Dog ownership is an area understood by most pupils, but an alternative area for discussion might be the right to own a cycle and to bring it to school.

This time, pupils could describe their responsibilities to other road users (including pedestrians) and to the school (where the bike is housed). The class might spend a lesson in small-group discussion on either of the above scenarios. A rights and responsibility charter might then be written up by each group for wall display.

The necessity of rules will have been explained by links to clearly understood examples like the rules of the road. A concept of what makes communities fair can also be expected at this level.

Because discussion is such an important learning tool in these two subjects, it should be made clear from the outset that all pupils are expected to make some contribution to it.

In learning about crime and the justice system, all pupils should develop a clear idea of just what it means to commit a crime. Pupils should also show some understanding of how criminals are treated within the justice system and how young offenders are treated differently from adults. Role play and the use of TV programmes are activities suggested by QCA for Key Stage 4 pupils learning about the criminal justice system (see www.standards.dfes.gov.uk and select 'Schemes of Work' and then 'Citizenship Key Stage 4, Unit 02).

The inclusive school teaches pupils *how to vote* by giving them the experience of doing so. It is important to recognise the basic principles of Parliament, and how elections work should be understood (e.g. campaigning to win votes). There should also be some recognition of the role of an MP and the tasks undertaken in office, even if this has to be explained at a basic level.

The notion of living in a diverse society is especially relevant to a school which prides itself on an inclusive approach. The aim should be to empower all pupils to describe their identities and their experiences of belonging to communities. Pupils should be able to understand that we are all part of different communities – locally, nationally and globally. One school did this by forming a partnership with the local parish council to address the effects of vandalism. A Merseyside school formed individual Internet links with English-speaking pupils in Holland, Spain and South America, looking at issues such as use of parkland. The curriculum should also aim to give pupils recognition that communities are interdependent.

How laws are made at a local, national and global level is an important concept with which the inclusive school should also be concerned. QCA literature cites the field of animal welfare as being suitable for discussing issues and giving examples of the importance of law. All pupils should be aware that there are differences of opinion over what the law should be in this regard and how it should be enforced. Pupils should know that laws are made and reviewed in Parliament, so some familiarity with Parliament is desirable.

Giving pupils a knowledge of what constitutes *local government* is also important, and a practical way of encouraging this is getting them to make suggestions as to how improvements can be made in the local area. All pupils should be able to demonstrate some knowledge of the services provided by local government (e.g. waste collection, road maintenance, libraries, etc.). A starting point here might be the school encouraging pupils to take responsibility by making opportunities available to manage areas of school life.

In helping pupils to understand the significance of *sport and leisure* in the local community, schools should seek to use actual issues in local life, and organise debates and discussions. There needs to be a recognition that such facilities are publicly funded, and pupils should identify how they themselves make use of them. The ability to suggest how provision and facilities could be improved should be developed in all pupils through good citizenship teaching. There should be some familiarity with laws and rules when they are applied to sports, particularly contact sports, and how the law steps in when rights are infringed.

The ability to research the *coverage of stories in different media*, the ability to discuss this, and to compare differing accounts, are expectations of all pupils at Key Stage 3.

Global citizenship is a concept which can be developed as a result of close collaboration between citizenship and geography. The accent should be on practical issues which can be researched and made graphic (such as deforestation of the Amazon rainforest or pollution of the oceans).

The development of a significant PSHE/citizenship vocabulary will be of considerable use. This can be built up in pupils' books and maintained in large-print wall displays in the areas where the subjects are taught. Keywords with which pupils should be made familiar from the outset should include:

> Rights and responsibilities, justice system, diversity, Parliament, local government, public services, election, voting, community, voluntary, conflict resolution, media, global.

A fuller list appears in Appendix 4.2.

How school atmosphere and events can support an active curriculum

There are a number of ways in which the PHSE and citizenship teacher can develop the school and classroom environment to better facilitate inclusion, but 'the right atmosphere' is likely to coincide with the 'least restrictive environment'.

'The right atmosphere' will be created through appropriate whole-school policies, the kind of policies that constitute citizenship in action, for example anti-bullying and equal opportunities policies, as well as clear guidelines for pupil participation. There must be confidence throughout the school that anti-bullying works and is not just a paper exercise.

If pupils are to become volunteers and willing 'doers' they need real opportunities to make decisions and take responsibilities that contribute to the running of the school and the management of their own learning.

- a pupil committee to select library books (from given choice)
- a pupil group to manage box office and ticket sales for school events
- pupil rota to show prospective parents and visitors round school (even when staff member is involved, pupils can always accompany to answer questions from a pupil point of view)
- older pupils can act as marshals for assembly
- pupils can manage car parking at special events
- a pupil cloakroom committee for productions and concerts
- pupils to act as ushers and programme sellers for concerts and plays
- pupils to co-present school assembly with staff

Appendix 4.3 provides a Year 7 lesson plan on 'Being a good and active citizen' and a Year 9 lesson plan on 'My future'.

Although this resource is by and large using discrete citizenship provision as its focus, it should be borne in mind that there are three other elements of provision cited by the DfES as contributory to its teaching:

- explicit opportunities in a range of other curriculum subjects;

- whole-school and suspended timetable activities;

- pupils' involvement in the life of school and wider community.

Can staff come up with a one-day event for a worthwhile charity which would be something to which *all* pupils could make a positive contribution? Could they also identify the charity which would satisfy most pupils?

Display as a tool for inclusion

In advising PSHE and citizenship teachers to invest heavily in wall and room displays, the context of the entire school building should be considered – from classrooms to corridors and from reception area to assembly hall. For example, the names of members of the school council should be clearly displayed in an area which is regularly visited by pupils. When voting procedures are being observed, posters should be displayed all over the school. If a particular topic – whether of global or regional significance – is the focus of citizenship lessons, then that too should be prominently displayed where all pupils will see it. Posters should be short and simple, with clear illustrations, and printed in large, bold font. In order to communicate clearly with pupils who have difficulties with literacy, there should be extensive use of illustration, bearing in mind that one picture can be worth a thousand words.

It should be remembered that conventional written communication may be inaccessible to some pupils with significant needs. In special schools and settings, symbols are used to great effect, and there is no reason why mainstream teachers should not take advantage of this alternative communication system. Many organisations produce their own symbol-supported materials which are circulated locally, and publications such as *Literacy Through Symbols* by Tina and Mike Detheridge have helped to spread good practice.

If you have wheelchair users in your class, remember to place displays at an appropriate height for them, as well as for everybody else.

Progressive schools have actually appointed small groups of pupils who take responsibility for wall displays, with the teacher acting as final arbiter in the choice of materials.

Bearing inclusion in mind when choosing appropriate textbooks

Choice of textbooks is something which departments will need to pay particular attention to when catering for an inclusive classroom. Good use of white space within the book is an essential, as nothing deters a pupil with poor literacy skills or a visual impairment like print overload. Clear and generous use of illustration, with no more than one topic or issue per page or spread is to everyone's advantage. (See Fig. 4.1 for guidance on design for handouts.) Where there are gifted and academically able pupils alongside non-academic youngsters, the teacher can always bring in supplementary texts. This need not be an expensive exercise, as daily newspapers and the Internet provide generous comment on the kinds of issues which are highlighted in citizenship lessons. Screen magnification software can be used to magnify the text on the computer screen. Teachers could also enlarge newspaper articles on the photocopier.

> Considering the criteria outlined above, which current textbooks used by the school best meet the needs of inclusion?

Fonts	Arial, Comic Sans, Sassoon and New Century Schoolbook are easier to read than other fonts.
Font size	12 or 14 is best for most pupils.
Font format	**Bold** is OK; *italic* is hard to read.
Spacing	Use double or 1.5 line spacing to help pupils who have problems with visual tracking.
Layout of materials	Use lots of headings and subheadings as signposts.
CAPITAL LETTERS	These are hard to read so use sparingly.
Consistency	Ensure instructions and symbols are used consistently.
Provide answers	If pupils can check answers for themselves, they learn more and become more independent.
Enlarging	It is better to enlarge text by using a bigger font on a word processor rather than relying on the photocopier. Photocopied enlargements can appear fuzzy and A3 paper never fits neatly in exercise books or folders.
Forms	If you are making an identity card or something similar, remember that partially sighted pupils often have handwriting that is larger than average, so allow extra space on forms. This will also help pupils with learning difficulties who have immature or poorly formed writing or are still printing.
Spacing	Keep to the same amount of space between each word. Do not use justified text as the uneven word spacing can make reading more difficult.
Alignment	Align text to the left margin. This makes it easier to find the start and finish of each line. It ensures an even space between each word.
Columns	Make sure the margin between columns clearly separates them.
Placing illustrations	Do not wrap text around images if it means that lines of text will start in different places. Do not have text going over images as this makes it hard to read.

Figure 4.1 *Producing your own materials – some guidelines*

How classroom layout can maximise the positive effects of inclusion

The layout of the classroom for PSHE and citizenship is particularly important because, above all else, it needs to support active learning. Row upon row of desks facing the teacher would be inappropriate, both in practical terms and in what this would communicate as a learning statement (which is not to say that there will not be some occasion to organise in this way). The room layout should communicate the idea that pupils learn from one another, that the teacher is a leader or facilitator rather than the fount of all knowledge and that face-to-face contact is an important feature of the learning.

For this reason, the circle or semi-circle has been developed by many PSHE teachers in the past as an excellent model for classroom layout. It is a clear statement that everyone matters and is expected to take part. Everyone in the class has a clear view of others which enables them to see and hear everyone's input clearly. There is no front and back where pupils can hide away or seek attention, so in this sense the circle is a perfect statement of equality of worth. Incidentally, both teacher and Teaching Assistants should take their place in the circle too. Everyone is included!

Another advantage of the circle is the fact that it is very easy to switch to small groups or to working in pairs. The only difficulty arises if pupils need to write, and this can be overcome by having available some art boards which pupils rest on their knees for scribing purposes. If the teaching room in question is dedicated to PSHE and citizenship, then all superfluous furniture could be removed. If the room is used for teaching other subjects, then the furniture should be light to lift and stackable, so that converting the room is a swift and relatively painless procedure. The room should be one with sufficient space for wheelchair users, and have good acoustics to minimise speech intelligibility problems for pupils with hearing impairment.

> Are PSHE and citizenship taught in the best possible classrooms? If not, what are the possibilities of relocating?

Overcoming the problems of storing records and data

The question of how pupils document their own learning or ideas is also worth considering. Although envelopes or wallets would appear to be the best format because they offer the most flexible option, using an exercise book should not be dismissed out of hand. There will be occasions when pupils are expected to make notes or jot down their own ideas as a result of group work, and exercise books are the obvious format. What they offer over the wallet idea is a coherent form which holds together the pupil's work in one document. It is much easier to impress upon the pupil that presentation and tidiness are important qualities of written work when that work is maintained in an exercise book. In short, encouraging the taking of pride in one's work is easier to reinforce when it is kept in one exercise book rather than in a number of sheets of paper which are maintained in a wallet or portfolio. Of course, there is no reason why pupils cannot be issued with both exercise book and portfolio.

Pupils can also use photographs taken with a digital camera, scanned into the computer and put into multimedia, desktop publishing or similar software, to document their achievements.

It must be borne in mind that evidence of achievement in PSHE and citizenship will arrive from a number of sources. Firstly, there will be the input of citizenship work in other curriculum subjects such as history, geography, RE, English, and so on. Secondly, there will be material from achievements within the school – posts of responsibility, academic and sporting achievements, and tasks such as peer mentoring, paired reading, etc. There may be externally awarded achievements such as ASDAN or the school's own certificates, which should be collected in the wallet. Finally, recommendations and achievements which a pupil has picked up in the wider community outside school should also be stored at school.

The principal problems associated with storing work in portfolios is keeping them tidy in appearance, ensuring that all evidence finds its way to the container, and developing some kind of indexing system within the portfolio. Clearly, under-pressure teachers are not in a position to supervise such a comprehensive task. It should be pointed out that taking responsibility for one's own actions and learning is one of citizenship's major educational aims, so developing pupil responsibility in the area of storing work and evidence is in keeping with this. Indeed, the QCA documentation goes further than this: 'The citizenship portfolio supports self-assessment and provides evidence for both formative and summative assessment during, and at the end of, the key stage.'

Much more will be included about recording, reporting and assessing in Chapter 6.

The inclusive school will have to cope with many youngsters who have both poor literacy skills and organisation skills. Where pupils would find this task beyond their individual responsibility, there will clearly need to be strong input from Teaching Assistants. However, schools should stop short of Teaching Assistants denying pupils responsibility for their own data collection and work organisation: this is contrary to the spirit of PSHE and citizenship and would constitute an inadequate preparation for the mastering of an important life skill. Good Teaching Assistants seek to develop organisational skills in the pupils they work with in order to equip them for life.

Working towards a more inclusive classroom environment in PSHE and citizenship may actually do the mainstream school a big favour in the area of recording and storing work. Because active learning is such an important principle in this curriculum area, it makes good sense to review what parts of the curriculum need written input and exactly what evidence needs to be stored. If thinking, speaking and participating are the key skills emphasised, then perhaps far less time needs to be spent writing notes which could be duplicated, handed out and subsequently annotated by pupils.

Is it possible to put the school's policy for collecting citizenship evidence on not more than one side of A4 paper?

The use of ICT to support an inclusive policy in citizenship

As pupils move towards the later parts of Key Stage 3 and into Key Stage 4, there is a strong research basis for elements of knowledge and understanding about topics such as human rights, the justice system, the civil courts, the media and global interdependence. Access to the Internet is important but, to pool the class resources effectively, it would make sense to book the ICT suite for a particular lesson or series of lessons.

The teacher prepares a list of websites relevant to the topic in advance and pupils can then work in pairs or small groups. The research task should be given a clear goal so that pupils can focus their thinking. Ensure that all pupils get their turn on the keyboard and establish turn-taking and co-operation as important principles from the outset (i.e. Year 7).

One important teaching point that needs to be borne in mind and dealt with very sensitively by staff is the fact that many of the non-academic pupils will need to develop these kinds of research skills to serve them as adults. The growth of the web as a tool for knowledge, opportunities and rights can only expand in the future. Seeing their peers access the Internet with ease and confidence and in a spirit of co-operation can only be of benefit to all pupils.

Would it be possible and of use to map pupils who have IT available at home?

Extra-curricular activities and inclusion

This would seem to be the appropriate point to consider taking part in citizenship outside the classroom. Working on reception duties, office support and as visitor guides are areas of opportunity which should be open to all pupils. Clear job descriptions by which pupils can measure their own performance is important. (See Appendix 4.4 for a sample jobs itinerary for a pupil working on reception duties.) Where a pupil may have difficulty coping alone, then they can be paired with others.

Organisation of school events such as parents' evenings, jumble sales and school productions can also be staffed by pupils. Such occasions offer clear opportunities for achievement certificates which can be stored in the citizenship portfolios.

If the school is to move towards an active democratic model, then the school council needs to have a clear constitution and budget as well as fair and proper elections. Turning the election day into a celebration of democracy and getting all pupils to vote will enhance school life.

Most schools now make use of the 'buddy' system whereby Year 8 pupils look after the induction of Year 7 pupils but the same philosophy can be applied when one pupil supports a peer with SEN. This can be extended so that Year 7s play a leading part in the link-up with the primary school. A great deal can be done to boost the confidence of new pupils through a successful liaison with their older counterparts. Linking up with feeder primary schools is particularly important as this passes on a positive approach to inclusion for future generations of pupils. Using activities such as environmental projects, mini sports days and cycling proficiency courses can provide occasions for fruitful liaison.

School or group events whereby a particular year comes off timetable for a day or half a day for a citizenship activity can be a positive force for inclusion. Celebrating human rights or a day on crime and safety awareness can appeal to all pupils and get them involved in the organisational aspect.

Fund-raising activities can also involve all pupils not just in the raising of money but in the administration and counting processes.

The careers exploration programme known as *The Real Game* (see http://www.becta.org), in which pupils work in groups of 15 to 20 to create a community which simulates issues and aspects of life that their parents and other adults meet up with in the real world, offers many positive openings for inclusion.

> Using the task sheet outlined in Chapter 6, is it possible to map out a pupil's progress through all 15 'acts of citizenship', given the school's present curricular and extra-curricular programmes?

In conclusion:

- The inclusive citizenship classroom is spacious and not cluttered with furniture or books. This will enable easy access for pupils and unimpeded movement about the classroom when the lesson switches from whole-class to group or pair work.

- The preferred seating arrangement for whole-class work is a circle or semi-circle with small stackable desks or art boards for writing purposes.

- The acoustics of an inclusive room have been maintained so that hearing-impaired pupils can clearly pick up the cues from the teacher and their peers.

- On the walls are key vocabulary terms as well as notices and posters which illustrate the issues which are encountered in the lessons.

- There is storage in the room for pupil portfolios (probably hanging files in filing cabinets), to which pupils have access at all times.

- In terms of atmosphere, it is a room which expects pupils to behave responsibly and always to respect other people's points of view.

I also believe that citizenship offers great opportunities to raise awareness amongst pupils about disability/difficulties, and quash some of the misunderstandings. Activities such as getting pupils to write while wearing thick gloves, read text backwards, and wear semi-opaque glasses can aid understanding of other people's difficulties.

Appendix 4.5 gives further lesson ideas for developing empathy with pupils with SEN.

CHAPTER 5

Teaching and Learning Styles

What makes citizenship and PSHE unique

The first and possibly most important thing that can be said about citizenship is that it is the one subject at which pupils really ought not to fail! (The same is true, of course, for PSHE.) Failure would imply that the pupil was a failure as a citizen (or as a person in the case of PSHE), and that would be a terrible stigma to lay on a learner.

The recognition that a pupil cannot fail in citizenship is what gives it such strength in terms of inclusion. It means that its practitioners do not need to sacrifice quality in the pursuit of quantity, as responsible citizenship recognises that all pupils are citizens, and support of each other is at the heart of responsible citizenship.

Although most of this chapter is dedicated to what goes on in citizenship and PSHE lessons, it needs to be stressed at the outset that if citizenship is to *work* in a school, it must prove itself more than a subject. Rather it will have an important bearing on a school's way of life, encouraging responsibility and participation at all levels as pupils mature into responsible citizens.

> How can the school's programmes in PSHE and citizenship be briefly summarised in a way which will reassure the parents of all pupils?

How citizenship is organised in the original Parliamentary orders

It is necessary to be fully conversant with the tripartite nature of the citizenship curriculum in order to maximise the benefits of inclusion.

The most substantial element of the curriculum comes under the heading of 'knowledge and understanding about becoming informed citizens' and it is largely this element we shall be addressing when we consider teaching and learning styles. However, pupils are also required to 'develop skills of enquiry and communication', and these skills are styled as 'thinking about', 'analysing' (largely ICT-based), 'justifying orally', 'writing', 'discussing' and 'taking part in debates'. In 'developing skills of participation and responsible action', the curriculum is dominated by active verbs – 'use their imagination', 'express', 'explain', 'negotiate', 'decide', 'take part responsibly' and 'reflect'.

What is very apparent from the two 'developing skills' areas is that active learning is the essential activity. It would be quite wrong then to proceed with a passive and writing-dominated approach to the element of knowledge and understanding.

What is being underlined at this point is that for inclusion to work successfully in citizenship, it is essential that teaching and learning be characterised by an active approach (which is not to say that there are not occasions upon which pupils become involved in passive learning).

> 'Active learning' is a frequently used term: brainstorm at least six working definitions of the term. Does any one term help more from an inclusion point of view than any other?

An active approach to becoming informed citizens

Most of the exemplar material presented in this resource is based upon the content of citizenship at Key Stage 3. This is for two reasons:

1   There is a formal assessment at the end of this key stage (as opposed to Key Stage 4 where there is not), which means that it encompasses the entire school population.

2   The content of the knowledge and understanding element of citizenship at Key Stage 4 is largely a development of the same headings.

Superficially, there are nine strands to the knowledge and understanding element of citizenship at Key Stage 3. It is worth recapping what they are in generic terms:

(a) rights and responsibilities, including basic aspects of the criminal justice system

(b) diversity of identity in the UK and the respect and understanding engendered through it

(c) central and local government and the services they offer

(d) parliamentary and other forms of government

(e) the electoral system and voting

(f) community-based, national and international voluntary groups

(g) the importance of resolving conflict fairly

(h) the significance of the media in society

(i) the world as a global community, the role of the EU, Commonwealth and the UN.

Although these nine strands make perfect sense as integers of understanding for an 'informed citizen', they look fairly challenging in terms of creating an active learning programme which promotes inclusion.

> Thinking in terms of pupils with learning difficulties, which of the topics under the heading 'knowledge and understanding' seem to be most and least user-friendly?

Teaching 'rights and responsibilities' to an inclusive class

There are many ways in which the teacher can explore rights and responsibilities (and the relationship between them), but it is imperative that pupils have a clear understanding of the terms and their reciprocity. The teacher should endeavour to make the language used as concrete as possible.

We may say, then, that *rights* are what a citizen is entitled to from a society. For example, a British citizen is entitled to a fair trial, free speech, education and a vote. Obversely, *responsibilities* are what a society is entitled to from its citizens. For example, a British citizen is expected to obey the law, pay taxes, etc. A basic sorting activity for this exercise is included in Appendix 5.1. For vision-impaired pupils, it may be necessary to photocopy this at 150 per cent. Given these definitions, pupils need to 'road test' them in a lesson which develops the skills identified as being key to citizenship.

The media, and newspapers in particular, feature stories which exemplify citizenship issues in an easy-to-understand way which also gives the lesson a grounding in 'real life'. The particular issue used for the following lesson was taken from a local evening newspaper, and gave substance to a powerful lesson about rights and responsibilities, which made important links to the criminal justice system.

Before the actual case history is presented, the teacher needs to clearly define what is meant by 'criminal responsibility'. This abstract idea can be presented in a way that non-academic pupils can understand (for example, by describing it as 'a person who has been involved in the committing of a crime').

In the story quoted below, the names have been changed.

MUGGER, 5, IS TOO YOUNG TO BE PROSECUTED

A child believed to be Britain's youngest-ever mugger has escaped prosecution because he is only five years old.

He and a nine-year-old friend were seen attacking a woman in her seventies. They tried to snatch her handbag. The attack took place at 1 pm last Sunday but fortunately the Johnson family came to the woman's aid and father Clive phoned the police on his mobile.

'We held on to the two boys, but they didn't seem bothered either by what they had done or by the arrival of the police,' said his wife Dawn. 'I even asked one of them how he would feel if it was *his* grandmother who was being attacked but he said he didn't care.'

The boys were arrested but police had to release them without charge because they were under 10 – the legal age of criminal responsibility.

Mrs Johnson was appalled: 'It is shocking that the law does not recognise them as criminals. Another 10 years on each of their backs and they will be hardened criminals unless this sort of behaviour is nipped in the bud.'

By asking capable readers within the class to present the story, everyone can have a clear understanding of the issues. The teacher could follow up the reading by outlining the main points of the story:

- the age of the offenders

- outsiders getting involved in the incident

- the police having to release the offenders because of their age

Like most successful citizenship lessons, this one is questions-based and, in order to involve all pupils, the majority of questions are as open-ended as possible.

The lesson could start with a 'thought shower' session considering the arguments for and against getting involved as an individual when pupils witness a crime such as robbery and assault.

Note that pupils are asked on this occasion to consider it from their point of view. This is an important ploy to get pupils personally involved. However, one of the dangers of such a ploy is that things get heated and social skills such as turn-taking can easily suffer. This is why the rules of debate and discussion need to be established at the outset of Key Stage 3 (if not before!). The teacher is doing her pupils a profound service if she instils positive procedural values in these important areas. Later in this chapter (under the heading 'Modelling Social Skills'), suggestions are offered as to how this might be done for pupils with learning difficulties.

To get the ball rolling if thought shower sessions are slow to start, the teacher can prompt contributions with carefully placed questions, e.g. 'In the story we have just listened to, what bad things could have happened to the family?'

It is possible that the responses could lead to a consideration of issues which last the entire lesson. If this is the case, the teacher should not feel unduly compromised by any apparent lack of progress. It cannot be emphasised enough that the inclusive citizenship classroom puts quality before quantity and that skills (such as discussion) are to be practised rather than written about.

Assuming the thought shower takes only a limited part of the lesson, the teacher could then split the class into four groups. The composition of these groups will have been carefully considered to balance abilities and difficulties, and to provide appropriate support where necessary. The groups can be maintained for a whole term/year so that pupils feel confident within them and can share roles such as spokesperson, secretary and discussion leader.

An activity sheet appears in Appendix 5.2 which frames the questions in a way which will enable groups to share thoughts and then use a scribe or secretary to record their impressions.

Using this 'rights and responsibilities' lesson as an example, the four questions facing the groups could be:

1   Should the boy's parents be prosecuted instead of him? If found guilty, what might be an appropriate punishment?

2   Suppose the boys had been ten years older, should the Johnsons have got involved? What should someone consider when deciding to 'have a go'?

3   Is ten years old a reasonable minimum age to be held legally responsible for your actions? If not, decide what is.

4   In the words of Mrs Johnson, how can this sort of behaviour be 'nipped in the bud'?

Another format which might prove more successful if many pupils in the class have undeveloped thinking skills, is to ask each small group to take the part of various factions in the story (e.g. police, the young mugger, the mugger's family, the lady who was attacked, neighbours of the lady). Each small group has a sheet of sugar paper on which they write words and phrases which can be used when it is their turn to express that character's point of view.

It should be emphasised that each group will 'report back' and that answers are expected for the questions they have tackled. When that report back occurs, the teacher needs to reinforce positive listening skills by encouraging a questioning process from the audience. Clear facial contact is vital if hearing-impaired pupils are to make progress in this procedural area.

The class could complete the topic through a role play whereby a policeman visits the mugger's parents. Either this could be done by each group, or the teacher could select the actors, who are then directed by the whole class, with the action being stopped periodically to allow instruction to be passed on.

Setting an appropriate homework assignment

One of the problems with whole-class and group work is that shy and reserved pupils can often go unnoticed. This may present particular problems for pupils with special needs who are reluctant to raise their heads above the parapet. Within citizenship, one possible redress is to set individual homework assignments which are designed in such a way that pupils can express their individual points of view.

For this unit, pupils could be given a photocopy of the newspaper article and asked to express in writing their own point of view on one of the four questions which were set for group work. It would be useful to set a minimum word limit as many non-academic pupils think that points of view can be expressed in one short sentence and are uncertain about how to expand their ideas. Furthermore, one principle which is vital to all citizenship lessons can be promoted through this kind of homework exercise: that all opinions are acceptable providing that they are reasoned. I can say something outrageous such as, 'I think blue-eyed people are more intelligent than brown' providing I can give a reason. Explain that backing an opinion with reason does not make it *the right opinion*, but it does make it worth arguing against!

> In setting homework assignments, think of ways in which parents can be used effectively to develop pupils' opinions and understanding.

A list of twenty suggestions for homework assignments is given in Appendix 5.3.

Teaching about diversity in a way which promotes inclusion

The theme of diversity is central to both citizenship and inclusion, but it is a massive area of study and, by its very definition, lacks homogeneity. It is especially important in an inclusive classroom for the teacher to give diversity a sharp focus. Taking a leaf from the book of child-centred education, the class can be introduced to the theme of diversity by using the pupils themselves as a starting point.

The teacher could explain to the pupils that he wants to build a profile of class members and to do this he would like each member of the class to provide a response to an itinerary of questions. This itinerary should then be displayed around the room using large letters and as much colour as possible so that the lesson remains inclusive to vision-impaired pupils. Ask all pupils to keep their answers to these questions as brief and to the point as possible (full sentences not necessary!) and to print their answers in large letters. Each pupil should make two copies of their answers, one of which will be for their own private use.

Profile questions

- What do you consider yourself to be able at (e.g. a school subject, football, skateboarding)?

- If there were only one TV show to watch, which would you prefer?

- What is your favourite smell (e.g. tar, petrol, a type of food)?

- Now select a taste you particularly enjoy.

- How would you describe your complexion (e.g. dark, fair, ginger, very light)?

- Think of something or somebody you love (e.g. pets, hobbies, objects, people).

- Think of someone in the media who you can't 'stomach'.

- Compared with the rest of the class, are you smaller, taller or average?

- Think of a characteristic of your feet (e.g. size, smell, fat, thin, flat, pointed, ugly, pretty).

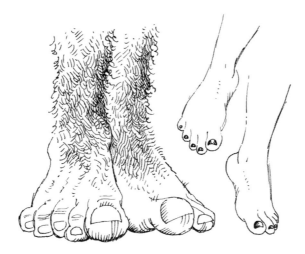

- The average family has 2.4 children, so how average is your family?

Each pupil is then given some Blu-Tack and asked to pin their profile on a particular wall. Encourage them to display at an appropriate height so that all pupils can see: it is easier to bend over than stand on a chair! The teacher then organises the class in such a way that everyone can visit the profiles of each classmate (one way to do this is to put male profiles on one wall and female on another). The main purpose of the exercise is for each pupil to identify the member of the class whose profile is closest to his/her own. The results will cut across friendships and gender differences, but the point needs to be made that the teacher might have constructed an entirely different profile which would have produced a completely different result.

The lesson has opened with an activity which includes everyone, breaks the ice, has a social basis and is sufficiently lightweight to relax class members. Their introduction to diversity has illustrated the fact that the differences between us, our own diversities, do not prevent nor promote friendships. It is often the differences between us which form the basis of our social lives.

The United Kingdom is a country that thrives on diversity, and defining British identity is a near impossible task, but it presents many intriguing possibilities for citizenship lessons.

> How can the question 'Who are the British?' be explored in a way which is meaningful to ALL pupils?

Considering diversity of language as a citizenship project

The following news article should be handed to each child. (It can be printed out, enlarged if necessary, from the accompanying CD.)

LONDON CHILDREN SHARE MORE THAN 300 LANGUAGES

London is the most linguistically diverse city on earth, researchers said yesterday after identifying 307 languages used by the city's children.

Only two-thirds of London's 850,000 children speak English at home. Most groups are from the Indian sub-continent, but there is just about a language for every letter of the alphabet from A for Abe (used in the Ivory Coast) to Z for Zulu.

In fact, there may be more than 307 languages because the number excluded many dialects and some London authorities had no records.

Dr Philip Baker said that London was even more multilingual than New York. At least 100 languages came from Africa alone, although some were spoken only by one or two children.

The Lord Mayor of London, Alderman Clive Martin, said the report showed why many leading organisations were basing their world HQs in London, but he called the problem 'a challenge to our education system.'

An activity sheet exists in Appendix 5.4 for the suggestions that follow.

For the lesson to proceed with full understanding, the teacher will need to revisit a number of terms in the news article which will have been handed to each pupil. 'Linguistically diverse' sounds very challenging to non-academic pupils so it needs demystifying by the teacher. The Indian sub-continent should be defined by reference to a wall map. Inclusive questioning through asking pupils to name a language to go with a letter (P? P for Polish; W? W for Welsh), will also ease understanding.

A full consideration of this example of diversity paves the way for forging a link between citizenship and thinking skills. The teacher could explain to the pupils the oft-expressed idea that a problem is an opportunity in disguise. The Lord Mayor cites one example of how 307 languages in one city presents an employment opportunity in that worldwide organisations build their headquarters in London because there is a workforce which is able to offer a wealth of languages. In their groups, pupils could be asked to make a list of possible jobs created because there are 307 languages spoken in London (e.g. charity organisations might choose to have their HQ in London). This is a demanding intellectual task for youngsters with learning difficulties, but if the teacher does some groundwork on the main employment areas served by language (print, conversation, audio), it should ease matters. Ideas could include interpreter services, CDs and books translated in different languages, telephone interpreters, restaurant menus, police interpreters for asylum seekers, etc.

The article goes on to describe the situation as 'a challenge to our education system', so pupils could be asked to list some of these 'challenges'. This could lead to a conversation about similar problems which might exist in the pupils' own school about youngsters speaking minority languages (e.g. in a subject like PE how do you ensure safety when safety depends on children understanding orders and their understanding of English is limited?).

Introducing the idea of cultural diversity

Teacher input could point out to pupils that language and skin colour are two ways of differentiating between people; can they think of another? The purpose here is to introduce the idea of culture (probably through dress being cited as marking out ethnic groups, along with language and skin colour). Again, starting at 'home' is a good idea; explain that culture is not fixed and teenage fashion exemplifies that point well (skateboards, BMX, baseball caps, etc.). Male and female outlines are offered in Appendix 5.5 so that pupils can build up their fictional teenagers on them. It may be useful to magnify these on a photocopier.

Each of the four groups could create a fictional teenager who is at the heart of teen culture (this could have been prepared for by asking pupils to bring in teen magazines). Encourage them to consider clothes, food, music, hobbies, objects and attitudes.

This creation could be through words and pictures, using original art or cutout, but it should be made clear by the teacher that the creation of the fictional teenager (including his/her name and age) is very much the responsibility of the whole group.

> How could an effective wall display on the theme of teenage diversity be presented?

Implications of practical work in citizenship for pupils who have special needs

Using art or low grade technology to make citizenship active is a good idea, providing the teacher remembers to include those class members who might have co-ordination difficulties. Organisation of the group as to who does what in advance or the judicious use of Teaching Assistants is called for. We have had one example of a piece of homework which supplements what pupils have been doing in class, but working on diversity offers an opportunity for pupils to do a piece of original research which can come together as a class project.

> What is the best way to make use of TA support in PSHE/citizenship lessons which make use of basic art and craft?

How to use research and the internet as a basis for homework

Explain that English is the most diverse language on the planet because it has stolen words from just about every language going. Ask pupils to do some original research by each finding 20 English words taken from other languages.

If there are 22 pupils in the group, they could create a Diverse English dictionary of 400+ words! Ask pupils to make use of the Internet using search engines as well as encouraging research in etymological dictionaries. Using a search engine like Google to discover adopted Spanish words (for example) produces useful websites. Bill Bryson's *Mother Tongue* also carries a chapter which could be simplified for pupils.

This task can be differentiated by the teacher holding a comprehensive list of basic words which non-academic pupils must research to discover the root language.

How the citizenship curriculum can have a bearing on the whole school

It is often difficult for young people to conceive of the size of planet Earth and, as a consequence, teaching about global interdependence issues presents a real challenge to teachers wanting to promote an inclusive classroom. And yet, with some careful preparation, it is possible to deliver lessons that are active, practical, inclusive and challenging.

By helping pupils to understand the global footprint as a metaphor, they can create some startling display work and become familiar with philosophical thought. Here is the basic metaphor that the teacher lays before the class:

> Think of yourself on a beach on holiday, wearing neither shoes nor socks. When you walk along the waterline you sink in slightly and make a footprint. In the same way, in the course of their lifetime, people make global footprints, leaving an imprint of everything they have consumed on earth – food, clothes, equipment, personal items, machinery, etc. The more they consume, the heavier the footprint, so a European will make a deeper global footprint than an African.

Working in pairs, the pupils are then challenged to create a rich and a poor person's global footprint. Given a sheet of sugar paper, one of each pair then takes off one shoe and draws round the outline of the foot. Using a bank of old magazines and newspapers to gather words and images, the pair then creates a rich and a poor global footprint by sticking their cutouts onto the foot outline. (These images can be overlaid and, if they spread beyond the outline, scissors will restore the outline at the end of the lesson.)

Pupils will find a wealth of images for rich people, but few for the poor. Pupils will ask questions about which words to use – particularly for the poor. Teachers can create rich and poor walls in the school's reception or assembly areas for a period during which the school focuses on poverty.

Some schools which have used the global footprint idea have found pupils asking challenging questions such as:

- Why is Africa so poor?

- Why is the Northern hemisphere richer than the Southern?

- Why do poor countries have such large families?

- Why is Aids worst in Africa? (Aids images make up many poor footprints.)

- What causes people to be rich and poor in the same country?

- What are the best ways for the rich to help the poor?

Figure 5.1 *Rich and poor footprints*

Working arrangements in class

Organising the global footprint project in pairs gives many opportunities to the teacher to make a positive use of the inclusive classroom. The pair can be seen as complementing one another's strengths or supporting one another in areas of difficulty. Because PSHE and citizenship are not concerned with linear curriculums which take pupils from point A to point B, it is quite legitimate for pupils to learn from one another. Not only is this an act of citizenship in itself, but the mainstream pupil actually learns about the process of learning. This applies to both intellectual and practical aspects of learning. Pairing also enables the Teaching Assistants to be used more flexibly for such a lesson on an 'as and when' basis.

Where the teacher uses small-group work, then it is useful to allow those groups time to work together, rather than shifting them round on a regular basis. This way individuals will get to know one another and the group will build up its own identity and self-help ethic.

Modelling social skills

Discussion is a skill that has to be taught to young people and it is a disappointing fact that many schools assume it is something which just happens. If our inclusive classroom is to be successful, then it needs to be taught from Year 7 onwards (actually it should be taught in primary school, but pupils arrive at secondary school in different states of readiness).

Observing the correct 'procedural values' was how the original working party on citizenship defined such education, and there are certain principles which need to be recognised in their pursuit.

Firstly, the speaker should be respected and listened to. Many successful teachers start by using an object which the speaker holds to show his/her privileged position at that particular time. Alternatively, there can be a show of hands which the teacher regulates. After a while, pupils may accept the simple raising of an index finger when they wish to make a contribution.

Another alternative is for the teacher to appoint a secretary from amongst the pupils (obviously someone with good literacy skills). It is the job of this person to note, in the correct order, pupils putting up their hands to make a contribution. The teacher can then allow each pupil to contribute at the right time.

No speaker should offer only an unsupported opinion: all ideas and opinions should be reasoned. The teacher, as discussion leader or chairperson, may need to bring out the reasoning for an opinion or, in extreme circumstances, rule out a contribution simply because it is unsupported opinion.

Members of discussion groups need to develop active listening skills. At any point, they should be able to summarise a given speaker's contribution. The teacher, as discussion leader, can promote active listening skills by briefly summarising speakers' contributions from time to time.

Finally, the discussion must move towards closure whether this be through a vote of the class on an issue (a great opportunity to demonstrate one member one vote), or through a meaningful summary by the teacher/discussion leader.

The ideal homework would be to ask pupils to do a brief written summary (say 100 words) of the discussion. Pairing can be used so that pupils with weak literacy skills can work with partners to create a joint summary.

Within the workings of a discussion, it is possible to observe the development of a number of social skills which support and promote inclusivity: turn-taking, active listening, participating in procedural values and respecting others' points of view.

> As a department, is it possible to frame a short, simple-to-understand document so that all pupils can comprehend the basic framework for a class discussion?

Linking performance management to citizenship/PSHE teaching

In considering performance management issues it is important to recall that citizenship is divided into three areas: (i) knowledge and understanding; (ii) developing skills of enquiry and communication; (iii) developing skills of participation and responsible action.

With regard to (i), a realistic target for a group of pupils might be that each member of the class could give an explanation of rights and responsibilities and the relationship between them. However, this is a long-term target and might have to be broken down into 'rights education' (Year 7), responsibility-taking (Year 8), and understanding the relationship between them (Year 9). Similarly, a basic target in Year 7 might be to develop in all pupils the ability to describe or define the media. This could develop into the analysis of a particular media product by each pupil as a SMART target over one term of Year 8.

Considering the developing skills areas in (ii) and (iii), performance management could consist of each pupil taking responsibility for certain citizenship acts which demonstrate achievement. In the following chapter – 'Monitoring and assessment' – an itinerary of citizenship acts which could be attempted in Key Stage 3 will be proposed. Teachers could identify single or small clusters of such 'acts' which are achievable in a time-limited way (e.g. week, term, year).

CHAPTER 6

Monitoring and Assessment

This chapter considers two different aspects of monitoring and assessment in citizenship and PSHE. First, there is the issue about how the teaching and learning within these 'subjects' will be monitored and assessed by Ofsted, and secondly (though not in importance) is how to monitor and assess the progress made by pupils.

In considering how Ofsted assesses citizenship, we need to look at core issues which affect inclusion as well as obtaining insights into assessing the pupils themselves.

With regard to assessing and monitoring individual pupil's progress, different circumstances apply from those which apply to most National Curriculum subjects. For example, SATs are not applicable, nor do pupils have to be given a level at either key stage. Instead, they are measured against end of key stage descriptions of attainment.

> The end of Key Stage 3 description approximates to levels 5 and 6 in humanities subjects. Is it possible and/or worthwhile to divide citizenship achievement between levels 5 and 6?

- How should schools handle the achievement of those pupils who do not manage the end of Key Stage 3 level of achievement?

- How can what pupils do (e.g. in the community, as service within the school) be balanced against what they know, to give a fair assessment?

What OFSTED says about monitoring citizenship

The Ofsted document makes it clear that the inspection focus will fall principally on designated citizenship lessons as well as other subjects which share objectives with citizenship. With regard to the latter, citizenship must turn up as a planned lesson objective rather than an incidental contribution. One of the main ways in which a teacher can make it clear that there will be citizenship elements in another subject lesson (e.g. history, English, RE), is to tell the pupils at the beginning.

Also important will be the contributions which occur outside the National Curriculum (for example, the pupils' school council). Here, there is an important passage regarding inclusion within the Ofsted document:

> Activities followed only by some pupils cannot meet requirements on citizenship unless suitable alternatives are available to all others. Where all pupils are involved in the school council process in a meaningful way, for example through discussion of issues in tutor groups and the election of representatives, this counts as part of the citizenship curriculum. However, a visit by a few individuals to a mayoral reception, in isolation, would not meet requirements.

Under the heading 'Standards and Achievement', inspectors are required to take into account pupils' starting points or capabilities, the progress they make over time and the demands made on them. One important admission is that 'in the early stages of implementation, progress over time may be difficult to ascertain'. Bear in mind that it will be 2007 when the first full cohort reaches the end of secondary citizenship.

The performance data which Ofsted uses will be internally moderated Key Stage 3 teacher assessments, GCSE results and 'other accreditation in citizenship'.

The actual work evidence which informs these assessments will:

> ... be drawn together from a variety of sources and may take forms other than individual books, files or artefacts. There may, for example, be products of collaborative work, or evidence in the form of photographs, local newspaper reports or video recordings. Minutes of a school council may give an indication of the quality of debate and the range of participation. Evidence might also be found in the form of Progress Files, community involvement and awards.

An itinerary of 12 questions which Ofsted inspectors will ask pupils gives an insight into the difficulties which inclusion might present. The wording of these questions has been slightly amended for brevity:

1 Even when the lesson is not citizenship, how do teachers of other subjects let you know that there is a citizenship element?

2 What is interesting and relevant in citizenship? Dull and irrelevant?

3 Does work in citizenship and PSHE make sense to you? Are there connections in subject content? Can you use skills from one lesson to another?

4 What opportunities are there for discussion and taking part in citizenship activities?

5 Have you been given responsibilities doing citizenship? What did you gain? Did you participate in decision making? Was there opportunity to work with others?

6 Are your views listened to? Can you contribute to the school council? How does it operate?

7 Do you get opportunity to discuss controversial issues such as politics and topical events?

8 Do you learn about different cultures present in the school/country?

9 Is there opportunity to discuss and challenge stereotypes (for example, with regard to gender and ethnicity)?

10 What sources of information are used in citizenship lessons?

11 What community activities have you been involved in? What were the activities about and what did you do?

12 How do you know what progress you are making? How is your work assessed?

One fillip for positive inclusion is the clear statement in the Ofsted document that 'evidence of participation in community-related activity is especially valuable'. In this regard, it is worth considering the third strand of the National Curriculum in citizenship which concerns the development of pupils' skills of participation and responsible action:

> It should be emphasised that this aspect of citizenship is also an integral part of the National Curriculum and that a school will fail to meet the requirements of the National Curriculum *if not all pupils take part*. There may, however, be opportunities for alternative experiences for different groups of pupils.

A Year 7 citizenship session in geography is considered as an exemplar lesson for this third strand of the citizenship curriculum:

> The mixed ability class has a small group of SEN pupils, including two with statements, is a broad ethnic mix and has a support teacher present. The pupils visit the local swimming pool which is currently closed and awaiting major rebuilding. The visit has been prepared for in preceding lessons and the site manager has been well briefed.
>
> The pupils question the site manager about the redevelopment and arrive with completed pupil questionnaires about the services they would like in the new pool. Their relevant questioning about the needs of the wider community goes down well and the motivation and confidence of the less able pupils, who clearly understand the issues, is evident.

'Methods of teaching that cater well for all pupils in the class' is mentioned under 'Teaching and Learning'. Teaching characteristics which are cited as bringing this about include:

- engaging pupils in discussion of issues which they see will affect their lives

- confident establishment of the context and ground rules for informed discussion

- encouraging pupils to think about controversial issues with sensitivity and objectivity

- providing opportunities to participate in and observe citizenship in action

- a balance between imparting information and encouraging pupils to enquire and research on their own account

- providing opportunities to communicate orally, in writing and by ICT

Recording progress in PSHE and citizenship can be viewed as a much more complex task than in other subjects, but this is more than compensated for by the fact that the teacher only has to match the evidence against an end of key stage description rather than give a National Curriculum level. What complicates the task of collecting the evidence is that it is drawn from so many different sources (e.g. input into citizenship from history, RE, etc., progress files, diaries), that the pupils themselves need to be involved in the recording and reporting processes, and that written work is one of many forms of admissible evidence. Pupils who are academically less able are likely to make greater use of oral and picture evidence, so it is important that school decisions about collecting information make the policy as wide ranging as possible.

Four favoured methods are citizenship diaries, online or written progress records or files, citizenship portfolios and pupil planners. To these we might add scrapbooks, which are a means of mounting photographs, newspaper reports and accreditations and awards from the wider community.

National Curriculum in Action records no fewer than 14 different sources of evidence of progress and attainment in citizenship:

- self-assessment sheets
- test results
- presentations
- photographs
- role play
- written work, such as investigations, research findings, reflective writing
- display work

- web pages
- participation diaries
- conference materials
- newsletters
- campaign materials
- teacher observation notes (including Teaching Assistant notes)
- peer observation notes

Collecting material in a portfolio allows pupils to build up a bank of evidence which is both formative and summative. The formative nature of portfolios makes them especially useful for inclusion. Where a conventional exercise or notebook may have glaring omissions when a pupil has not been present, a portfolio is of a quite different nature and offers at least four advantages by involving the pupil in:

- setting criteria for what they want to achieve and what they might include in the portfolio

- reviewing evidence collected against the criteria at regular points during the year or key stage

- reflecting on the nature of evidence selected and how it demonstrates progress made in developing skills, knowledge and understanding

- selecting pieces of evidence to demonstrate achievement, and giving reasons for choices, as part of summative assessment for example, at the end of year or key stage

How can progress over time (say an academic year) within a school's citizenship programme be assessed? In this task, it may be useful to focus on development of concepts and procedural information rather than knowledge content. For example:

- Does a pupil have a notion of democracy?
- Does a pupil stick up her hand every time he/she wishes to make a contribution?
- How can a pupil's individual progress be assessed for the same spell of time?
- How will pupil evidence be stored and made available for Ofsted inspection (bearing in mind the need to collect individual portfolios and evidence of community events)?

Including pupils with learning difficulties in PSHE and citizenship

The QCA PSHE and Citizenship Handbook (QCA/01/749), which is concerned with teaching and assessing the curriculum for pupils with learning difficulties, offers particularly worthwhile advice.

There are four areas of opportunity which are offered to pupils with learning difficulties:

1 making choices and decisions

2 developing personal autonomy by having a degree of responsibility and control over their lives

3 making a difference or making changes through individual and collective action

4 finding out there are different viewpoints which lead to a respect for the opinions of others

The path for progress using these opportunities in PSHE and citizenship is one whereby pupils move from a narrower to a wider perspective: moving from school to community; from personal to other people's points of view; and from immediate to future time (for example, coming to realise how tackling things differently could lead to different outcomes).

Strategies for modifying the Programmes of Study for pupils with learning difficulties

Four important strategies are offered as ways of modifying the Programmes of Study for pupils with learning difficulties:

- choosing material from an earlier key stage or more than one key stage (which effectively means that a Key Stage 3 youngster with learning difficulties can be directed towards related material at Key Stage 1 or 2). For example, Ingrid Oliver in her *Scholastic* publication *Ready to Go: Ideas for PSHE – KS2*, develops an idea which she terms 'Shipwrecked!' In this exercise, pupils organise a society and prioritise. It is an excellent way of introducing older pupils with learning difficulties to rights education, notions of trade, justice and government;

- reinforcing and generalising previous learning while introducing new knowledge, skills and understanding;

- using the PSHE framework and the citizenship Programmes of Study as a resource *which is appropriate to the age and needs of pupils*;

- focusing on one aspect or a limited number of aspects of the age-related guidelines.

Arguably the most informative and useful sections of this handbook are those which suggest modifications to the guidelines and Programmes of Study for pupils with learning difficulties.

PSHE at Key Stage 3

As far as PSHE at Key Stage 3 is concerned, the focus of teaching becomes tighter and a trio of opportunities is suggested:

1 Learn about the nature of friendships and relationships, including sexual relationships.

2 Recognise the risk in some situations, making safe choices and communicating the need for, or refusal of, help.

3 Appreciate what makes a healthy lifestyle.

Assuming these opportunities are made available through the school's Programme of Study at Key Stage 3, the handbook usefully identifies what is achievable by those with learning difficulties.

All pupils, even those with profound disabilities, are thought able to:

> Continue to develop awareness of themselves and their bodies by approaches and contexts appropriate to their age. They have support to meet new challenges and to cope with transitions in school life. They make or are helped to make choices.

Most pupils with learning difficulties, including those with severe learning difficulties, can:

> Become more mature and independent. They take on a greater responsbility for themselves and become more aware of the views, needs and rights of others. They learn to cope with their changing bodies and feelings and with changing relationships. They recognise that there are risks in some situations.

A few pupils with learning difficulties:

> Learn new skills in making decisions. They have the opportunity to use their developing personal power responsibly, and to make choices about their health and their immediate environment. They make informed decisions about their future.

Citizenship at Key Stage 3

Two key focal points emerge as being applicable to all pupils in citizenship:

1 Take a full part in the life of the school and become involved in making decisions.

2 Express their opinion on topical issues.

Given these opportunities, the handbook defines the following possible achievements in citizenship:

All pupils with learning difficulties (even those with the most profound disabilities):

> Continue to take part in the life of their school community. They make, or are helped to make, their views known on issues important to them.

Most pupils with learning difficulties (including those with severe difficulties in learning) will develop further skills, knowledge and understanding in most aspects of the subject. They will be able to:

> Express their opinion on topical issues. They learn about fairness and diversity at school and in the community, for example by taking part in community activities.

A few pupils with learning difficulties who will develop further aspects of knowledge, skills and understanding in the subject:

Think about and discuss topical issues, problems and events; listen to others' views; and learn how to become more effective in public life. They learn about some legal, political, religious, social or economic issues and about fairness and diversity at a local and wider level.

PSHE at Key Stage 4

At this point it is appropriate to consider the further expectations for pupils with learning difficulties which apply at Key Stage 4.

The PSHE focus is more tightly defined:

1   Prepare for adult life by thinking about post-16 choices available.

2   Be aware of their personal qualities, skills and achievements.

3   Deal with changing relationships.

All pupils with learning difficulties (even those with profound disabilities):

Continue learning about themselves as young people and members of their communities. Continue to develop awareness of themselves and their bodies by approaches appropriate to their age. With support, they prepare for transition to adult life. They make their views known about their decisions through self advocacy or advocacy.

Most pupils (including those with severe difficulties):

Take greater responsibilities in preparation for adult life. Are encouraged to learn how to cope with a wider range of relationships and to respect the views, needs and rights of people of all ages. Have opportunities to make choices about their future. Know where to obtain help and understand some ways of dealing with risky situations.

A few pupils with learning difficulties:

Learn how to plan for their future and their careers by setting personal targets and begin to consider the consequences of their decisions. Develop skills to help them actively seek information and advice and deal with changing relationships in a positive way.

Citizenship at Key Stage 4

Two focal points are suggested for citizenship at Key Stage 4:

1   Find out about and be part of their local community.

2   Learn about a political or economic system (e.g. a bank, the electoral system).

Note how the opportunities to be made available at Key Stage 4 have progressed significantly from Key Stage 3:

All pupils with learning difficulties (even those with most profound disabilities):

Have opportunities to take part in the life of their school and local community. They learn about the diversity of people's lives (e.g. family relationships, lifestyles and cultures).

Most pupils with learning difficulties (even those with severe disabilities):

Think about and take part in discussions on topical issues, problems and events. They have opportunities to learn about legal, political, religious and social or economic institutions. They receive the support they need to understand that their expressed views or their actions can bring about change.

A few pupils with learning difficulties:

Learn about legal, political, religious, social and economic systems. They are helped to develop greater knowledge and understanding of topical issues and to take part in discussions and debates.

Of course, it is not possible to legislate just how far into the citizenship curriculum a school can go with a particular pupil who has learning difficulties. These are decisions which can only be made at school level through negotiation between the SENCO and the subject specialists. Certainly, *The PSHE and Citizenship Handbook* has many practical and realistic suggestions about organising an active Programme of Study for pupils with learning difficulties.

Appendix 6.1 contains several secondary case studies involving pupils with SEN studying citizenship.

> How can the school build up a bank of learning materials which modify Programmes of Study for pupils with learning difficulties according to the four strategies outlined in the Ofsted handbook?

Developing a method of self-reporting for all pupils in citizenship

> Working out a meaningful learning programme in PSHE and citizenship for all pupils is a complex task in its own right, but how does the school link that to the important element of self-reporting and assessment which is seen as being such an integral part of both subjects?

One method which could prove successful to schools committed to inclusion is presented here in the form of a task sheet (see Figure 6.1). The contents of this sheet are not set in stone, indeed teachers would be encouraged to adapt the list of 'acts of citizenship' according to the learning programme in PSHE and

ACTS OF CITIZENSHIP

ACT	TICK BOX	BRIEF DESCRIPTION
1. Be a good neighbour		
2. Contribute to the community		
3. Contribute to a discussion		
4. Counsel someone in need		
5. Express a reasoned opinion		
6. Help a charity		
7. Identify a political issue		
8. Lead a small group		
9. Negotiate to end conflict		
10. Research an issue using IT		
11. Show organisational ability		
12. Speak to an audience		
13. Support a friend		
14. Take my own responsibility		
15. Volunteer for a task		

Please note: ONE activity can be used as an example of NO MORE THAN TWO acts of citizenship.

Figure 6.1

citizenship of a particular class/individual. The basic inventory as it is presented should serve to cover the whole of Key Stage 3 for the majority of pupils.

Simplicity is the key note, both in terms of defining the task carried out by the pupil and the recording and collection of how the task was done as a piece of data. It is not unrealistic to expect most pupils to meet all 15 'acts of citizenship' within the three years of a key stage. For a pupil with severe learning difficulties, it could be trimmed to ten tasks. For a youngster with profound learning difficulties, there is no reason why five tasks could not be substituted.

The description of the act should be kept as brief as possible and need not necessarily be written by the pupil, but it should be dated and authenticated by a person who was witness to its execution (in the form of signing or initialling). This person could be a fellow pupil, a parent or an adult living in the community.

So, for example, 'be a good neighbour' could be described thus: 'I went shopping with my parents and bought groceries for our neighbour.' The neighbour for whom the pupil shopped could be the signatory.

'Contribute to the community' might be described as: 'I was in a small group who litter-picked the road outside our school.' For this example, the teacher or another member of the litter-picking group could provide the signature (pupils are encouraged to be an integral part of the recording process).

There are many ways of collecting evidence and the medium of digital photography allows teachers to build up an impressive wall display of citizenship in action, as well as allowing individual pupils to record their work in a simple and effective way. Software programs like Via Voice enable pupils to speak into a computer about their acts of citizenship which the computer will then write up as sentences (although there has been some difficulty in terms of voice recognition and hearing impaired pupils with this resource).

As the key stage progresses, the gaps in this inventory will make it clear to pupils what their learning targets need to be.

Although this approach does not accord with the end of Key Stage 3 description (which is heavily reliant upon the 'knowledge and understanding' aspects of citizenship), it could be used to give a 'spine' for work completed by pupils in their progress files.

Of course, the obvious implication of adopting a criteria-led approach is to plan the PSHE and citizenship curricula in such a way as to give pupils the opportunity to meet those criteria. Certainly, as far as pupils with special needs are concerned, it cannot just be left to chance that those criteria will be met.

When it is impossible to match a pupil with an end of key stage description

In order to get schools to take citizenship seriously, and in order to invest it with something approaching academic rigour, the decision was taken at the highest level to give it statutory powers. What this meant in effect was that rather than ask teachers to give pupils a National Curriculum performance level, it was decided to match pupil performance against end of Key Stage 3 and 4 attainment descriptors (bear in mind that the end of Key Stage 3 approximates to levels 5 and 6 in other National Curriculum subjects).

Almost immediately, teachers and educators objected to this approach. Suppose it proved impossible to match a pupil against either of those descriptions, did that mean that the pupil would be seen as a failed citizen? The notion was clearly ludicrous, but it has not stopped examination bodies from coming up with short course GCSE citizenship which still begs the same question. (Because PSHE is based on guidelines and is non-statutory the same problems do not arise in this area of the secondary curriculum.)

Fortunately, performance descriptions (or P scales as they have come to be known) have been created for pupils whose linear progress has still not yet taken them to attainment at National Curriculum level 1. Performance descriptions work on a 'best fit' basis, which means that a pupil's performance over a period of time and in different contexts is measured against specific P scales within PSHE and citizenship. Although performance descriptions exist from P1 to P3, their nature is so generic that it is impossible to disentangle elements which can be identified as belonging to PSHE or citizenship.

Consider then P4, the lowest level at which elements of PSHE and citizenship can be discerned:

P4 Pupils express their feelings, needs, likes and dislikes using single elements of communication (words, gestures, signs or symbols). They engage in parallel activity with several others. Pupils follow familiar routines and take part in familiar tasks or activities with support from others. They show an understanding of 'yes' and 'no' and recognise and respond to animated praise or criticism. They begin to respond to the feelings of others.

There is almost no facility within this description for assessment of unsupported work of an academic and/or written nature. The implication is that a pupil who would be assessed on level P4 might be the same age as pupils studying citizenship at Key Stage 3, but would have a learning programme taken from citizenship at Key Stage 1, or even PSHE tasks described in handbook QCA/01/749 under headings like 'developing personal autonomy' and 'personal care'.

By the time a pupil has progressed to **P8**, the performance description is significantly more sophisticated:

P8 Pupils join in a range of activities in one-to-one situations and in small or large groups. They choose, initiate and follow through new tasks and self-selected activities. They understand the need for rules in games, and show awareness of how to join in different situations. They understand agreed codes of behaviour which help groups of people work together, and they support each other in behaving appropriately, for example while queuing in a supermarket. They show a basic understanding of what is right and wrong in familiar situations. They can seek help when needed, for example assistance in fastening their clothes. They are often sensitive to the needs and feelings of others and show respect for themselves and others. They treat living things and their environment with care and concern.

When we consider this far more detailed description, it relates more closely to work done at Key Stage 1 than any other point of the PSHE/citizenship curriculum, but even then it has to be remembered that work done at Key Stage 1 would take most pupils to the equivalent of levels 1 and 2 in terms of National Curriculum. This would represent a significant achievement for many pupils with SEN. It is worth noting the four expected outcomes of knowledge, skills and understanding which apply at Key Stage 1 to understand how they would help to generate the **P8** assessment outlined above:

- developing confidence and responsibility and making the most of their abilities

- preparing to play an active role as citizens

- developing a healthy, safer lifestyle

- developing good relationships and respecting the differences between people

The role of citizenship and PSHE in the IEP process

It is unusual for citizenship and PSHE to be cited specifically on an IEP – but that does not mean that they do not have a part to play in a pupil's action plan. Certainly, where behaviour modification is concerned, skills learned in PSHE can play a significant part in a pupil's targeting. (See sample IEPs provided in Appendix 6.2.)

The lines of action to be followed by Care/Action Plans are common to all schools; there is, however, no set pro forma. To illustrate the possible applications of PSHE in the Care/Action Plan of a statemented youngster, consider the example of a plan given in Appendix 6.3 which is taken from a school in the north of England. All names have been changed in order to retain anonymity.

Considering first the Care/Action Plan outcome measure, the initial evaluation on John offers scope for work in PSHE. Although he is an aggressive Year 8 with a record of damage to property, his transfer to and inclusion at a new mainstream secondary school has had a positive effect upon his behaviour. The anxiety John presents along with low self-esteem is an area that PSHE as a subject could target. It is feasible that at Year 8 level, South School will include work within its PSHE programme on improved self-esteem and even if this proves not to be the case, the department could advise the SENCO on how to approach this goal.

As far as John's awareness that he is 'very different' from other youngsters goes, the theme of diversity within the citizenship programme represents an opportunity for the school to work on the acceptance of all members of the school community. Also there is an active and successful buddy scheme in operation to which John could subscribe.

The action element of this outcome measure targets direct one-to-one work on the 'I am special' package/anger management. This impinges upon the 'conflict resolution' theme which can surface in all three years of Key Stage 3 citizenship.

In the second part of the Care/Action Plan, John's own action plan, our focus is on target 2 – 'to avoid losing my temper'. The five bullet points that John has settled on all have implications for PSHE and the final point – his resorting to a trusted friend during difficult times – could well be supplemented with a unit of pair work around the theme of conflict resolution.

Considering the third part of the Care/Action Plan – a summary of John's progress, difficulties and objectives as well as the staff action plan – there are also implications for the school's PSHE and citizenship department. Two of John's major objectives are directly associated with its work:

- improve social communication skills

- improve self-control and anger management

An active and interactive programme amongst all Key Stage 3 pupils will not only benefit John immensely because of what he learns, it will benefit the pupils with whom he has contact who can master the skills needed to cope successfully with John.

What PSHE and citizenship can offer pupils such as John is not only support within the classroom and learning situation for him as an individual, but support for his peers. Their co-operation and understanding will be vital if South School is to make a success of his inclusion. A committed PSHE and citizenship department really can make a difference to the environment and atmosphere of the school and to the attitudes of the pupils in it.

Managing Support

Citizenship and PSHE are two subjects rather than one

In planning and managing support, teachers of PSHE and citizenship need to bear in mind that the range of different working situations which pupils are likely to meet in these subjects is considerably wider than in most other curriculum areas. Additionally, when the department is committed to an active learning programme (and in PSHE 'active' is likely to mean just that!), the demands on the Teaching Assistants are likely to be all the greater.

What makes pupil support in PSHE and citizenship so valuable

Although TAs will be used to help pupils with difficulties in written work in PSHE and citizenship, generally they will need to exhibit greater flexibility and wider adaptive skills than in other subjects.

Subject knowledge is probably less esoteric and academic than other curriculum areas, but this in itself can present problems for the teacher. For example, if pupils are doing a lesson on elections there is a danger that the TA may assume that the everyday knowledge she possesses on the subject equips her to pass on information to the pupil. But the teacher's main objective may have more to do with 'procedural values' than knowledge of the topic. The lesson's main learning points may be achieved through the pupils doing an actual vote in a ballot box rather than increasing their knowledge base about elections.

The importance, therefore, of the teacher communicating the lesson's main objectives at the outset (if not in advance of the lesson) should be apparent. (See Appendix 7 for an example of advance information which would assist TA input in a citizenship lesson.)

If the departments have a commitment to developing skills within discussion and debating and working in more flexible classroom formats, the TA will need to develop appropriate skills to know when to intervene and when to learn from observation. She may have to mediate when things threaten to break down in pairings or small groups, or at least bring the threat of breakdown to the teacher's attention.

Using the circle or semi-circle for discussion and general oral work puts a pressure on the TA to get involved, for there can be no observers in such a classroom arrangement, only participants. However, the TA must take care not to grab any of the limelight in such a role.

Clearly, working more in a social capacity than in most other lessons, the TA is an invaluable member of the team, feeding the teacher with vital insights which will enrich the learning experiences of all pupils.

Helping the TA cope with the demands of secondary PSHE

Valuable time needs to be spent on helping TAs to become familiar with the guidelines of PSHE at Key Stages 3 and 4. The areas to be covered are, as the subject title would imply, personal and social. Immediately, this communicates the fact that the work done by the Teaching Assistant will need to be executed sensitively and carefully. Many of the pupils with special needs with whom TAs deal have problems which are either personal or social and probably both, so dealing in a subject which focuses on these areas is bound to be a sensitive area.

According to the subject guidelines, the personal and social issues which are to be taught are arranged under three headings:

- developing confidence and responsibility and making the most of their abilities

- developing a healthy, safer lifestyle

- developing good relationships and respecting the differences between people

Of course, these are overall key stage objectives and will be broken down by the subject teacher into more manageable short-term goals. For example, under the first of these headings pupils should be taught:

> ... to recognise the stages of emotions associated with loss and change caused by death, divorce, separation and new family members, and how to deal positively with the strength of their feelings in different situations.

All manner of personal difficulty and trauma could be uncovered through teaching on these themes, and it is likely that supported pupils will have been more traumatised than most. The Support Assistant may well have to step outside his/her normal remit to deal with problems which may arise. Such delicate personal issues can only be referred to in general terms in whole-class situations, but that does not preclude direct one-to-one work between pupils and between a pupil and a TA.

Helping the TA cope with the demands of secondary citizenship

TAs need to realise at an early stage that the knowledge and understanding element to be taught in citizenship at Key Stages 3 and 4 is less personal than work in PSHE. Consequently, the work of the TA is likely to be demanding in terms of knowledge of the subject area and ability to marshal resources for practical tasks. The danger here is that TAs might assume their own 'street knowledge' of issues such as Parliament and the media will suffice. Certainly it will help, but teachers need to spend time outlining what is to be covered and the main learning points which will be made. There are numerous possibilities – from giving the TA advance access to the teacher's lesson notes to marking out in a textbook the basis of the next lesson. The TA team within a school can build up a resource of PSHE and citizenship materials.

The TA is also likely to have an important role in helping pupils to collect material for their citizenship portfolio (more will be said of this later in the chapter).

Just as important as citizenship's knowledge and understanding are the requirements to:

- develop the skills of enquiry and communication

- develop skills of participation and responsible action

It may be useful here to raise the issue of TAs sometimes allowing/encouraging pupils to become dependent on them – when their role should be to make the pupils as independent as possible. Once again, it is the good judgement of the TA which is at issue. Simply telling a pupil that they must now manage without help may produce a negative reaction. It may be more appropriate to help set up a task and warn in advance that from a certain point a pupil will be on his or her own. Making it clear to the pupil that 'going it alone' is an important aspect of learning will be reinforced if the TA does effective follow-up: lots of praise where appropriate, advice where things have faltered.

The first of these 'skills' areas may involve the Learning Support Assistant in helping with research through use of the Internet and by searching the shelves of the school library. Encouraging a pupil to make an oral contribution may involve the TA listening to numerous rehearsals of speeches: the sounding board role is a particularly important one.

The second developing skills area may involve actual work in the community or promoting inter-pupil negotiation and discussion. The TA may well become an arbiter when pupils find it difficult to negotiate a satisfactory outcome.

The most important aspects of a supportive role

PSHE and citizenship are usually taught in mixed-ability groups and this presents a challenge for the TA, who will be a key figure in the fostering of peer group acceptance. Getting other pupils to accept and value the supported pupil by sensitively drawing attention to their skills and achievements is an important part of the role. At times, the TA may have to intervene by making the pupil take a leadership role in appropriate activities and persuading others to accept this.

There are all kinds of ways that a TA can help an included pupil who has limited social skills. Where the occasion allows (for example, the TA may know in advance from the teacher what situations are likely to occur in a lesson), the TA can practise the skills required *before* the lesson. Much more tricky but no less worthwhile is practising social skills *after* things have gone wrong. Questions such as:

- How could you have done that better?

- Why do you think people misunderstood what you said?

- Could you have listened more carefully before you spoke?

may have to be presented to the pupil once the TA judges that they are able to deal with the issues.

Simply listening to a pupil (another example of the 'sounding board' role considered at length below) is especially important when he or she wants to discuss feelings or issues about right and wrong.

When a pupil performs creditably in PSHE, it is very important to give encouragement and praise because this will do so much to build self-esteem and confidence. Being either too 'general' or 'gushing' with praise may well prove counterproductive, though. Picking out the specifics of what the pupil did well enables them to strategise for the future.

In Glenys Fox's *Handbook for Special Needs Assistants* there is an excellent piece of advice on developing listening skills:

> When you start working with a pupil, it is tempting to do a lot of the talking and to expect that the pupil has taken in what you have said. Remember that effective communication is a two-way process and that some children need time to get their thoughts together and to express themselves. Some are only able to understand short bits of information at a time. You may need to check out that the pupil has understood by asking him or her to repeat back to you the information you have given.

It is important that TA's develop their own listening skills, but they are also in a position to help pupils develop theirs. Full attention when listening, good eye contact, backed up by nodding and smiling in the right places, will give the appropriate non-verbal messages. One way to approach a pupil in a listening situation is to treat them rather like a journalist might approach someone to be interviewed for a newspaper column, asking appropriate open-ended questions in the right places, and carefully reflecting back what you think has been said.

The Teaching Assistant will see the effect of a lesson in PSHE and citizenship in micro terms where the class teacher is more likely to consider the macro (whole-class) consequences. There are two implications from that realisation.

The first is to recognise the importance of a lesson's objectives and main learning points. If the method of learning chosen by the teacher does not work for a pupil, then the TA may be in a position to get there by another path. The second is the role of the TA as a supplier of information to the teacher about how well the pupil is coping with the demands made on him or her. The teacher can make all kinds of fine adjustments to future lessons as a result of that information.

The importance of the TA's role in monitoring and assessing citizenship

Recording the work TAs have done with pupils is an essential part of their commitment, and between the class teacher and the school SENCO they need to be advised about what sort of records to keep. The information required may be pupil-specific and/or subject-specific. An evaluation of how well the pupil learned doing a particular activity will help the subject teacher for planning purposes.

Most schools will be using portfolios as a means of pupils looking after their work in citizenship. The reason for this is to do with the fact that evidence comes from various sources:

- PSHE and citizenship lessons

- other subjects which contribute to citizenship

- tutor group (for services in and around the school)

- the wider community

As has been mentioned in the previous chapter, some included pupils will have poor organisational skills, and this means they will need assistance in this area. However, improving these skills so that pupils can take their own responsibilities is one of citizenship's primary objectives. This does not mean that the Teaching Assistant should refuse to help a pupil who is obviously struggling with putting together a portfolio, but rather that the Assistant should help in a way that enables the pupil to take their own responsibility in the future. There are all kinds of ways of doing this:

- encouraging the pupil to take notes about how a task is done

- asking them to talk through how the task was done

- planning in advance for the next task

Difficulties may arise when there is an element of self-assessment to work in citizenship, and the TA may need to explain criteria which can be used as a mcans of developing self-assessment.

The relationship between PSHE / citizenship departments and their TAs

Sadly, many schools view the PSHE and citizenship departments as the poor relations because they do not have examinations at the end of the course (although with the introduction of short course GCSE in citizenship, it will be interesting to see what kind of effect that has on that perception). The reality is that mixed-ability groupings in PSHE can take strength from the lack of exam pressure and make real strides in developing social skills. To do this effectively, the teacher needs to be supported, especially where teaching groups are 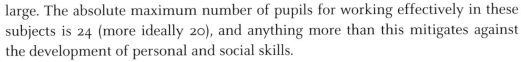 large. The absolute maximum number of pupils for working effectively in these subjects is 24 (more ideally 20), and anything more than this mitigates against the development of personal and social skills.

Creating a secure framework for the lessons, where Teaching Assistants can use their own initiative but feel comfortable with their knowledge of what is to be taught, will help to ensure success. Making them aware of how they are valued will create a situation where TAs want to come back for more – an important issue when choices have to be made about where support can be offered! In the best situations, TAs can become passionate supporters of the work you do, and useful allies!

Helping TAs to review, evaluate and improve their performance will require an input from the teacher in the form of a clear explanation about:

- the lesson structure

- the main skills and/or knowledge to be imparted

- the key areas for TA help

On this basis, TAs can measure their own performance. For example, the key area for help could be encouraging a pupil to make a greater contribution to the class discussion. The teacher could point out the opportunities to help the pupil within the lesson and the intended path of progress for the discussion. This knowledge will help the Assistant to develop a strategy and a means of considering how successfully that strategy was met.

Helping the TA to develop their abilities in PSHE and citizenship

Enquiry, discussion and social skills are key areas within these two subjects and, as a result, the pupil is likely to meet a wide array of different learning situations.

There will be occasions when, in the TA's judgment, it is important to follow up some aspect of learning with a review. It could be about an inadequate or inappropriate response, about an undeveloped social skill in need of attention, or a generally unacceptable classroom performance. The TA's judgment is paramount here in making the decision about further action.

Having made a decision to follow up an issue which needs attention, it may be necessary to apportion some time later in the day. Maybe this issue is so important that it ought to take priority over a less demanding learning situation in the timetable. At least holding the meeting at a special time communicates the message that this is viewed as an important issue. The TA would need to go into such a meeting with a clear strategy, possibly arrived at following discussion with the teacher in whose lesson the issue arose.

Judith is very disappointed with Shaheem's poor participation in a class discussion (which she supported). She makes notes on three principal areas of concern regarding Shaheem's behaviour:

1 speaking to the teacher with lack of respect
2 shouting out answers rather than putting his hand up
3 having a private joke with another pupil

Shaheem reports back 20 minutes before the end of the lunch break. TA explains that she is unhappy with Shaheem's behaviour in citizenship without going into detail. Asks Shaheem for his own observations. Then deals with each area of concern individually, asking Shaheem to account for his actions.
If Shaheem is contrite, TA helps him to write a letter of apology. If Shaheem is unrepentant, a meeting is arranged with the SENCO.

As with teachers, there are TAs who are naturally equipped to succeed and there are others who need to refine and improve what they do as a result of reflecting upon their own practice. This latter group can learn much from watching other TAs and teachers in action, but there need to be programmes in place which *ensure development* rather than simply let it occur by chance.

These programmes would need to include features such as:

- training in the issue of confidentiality

- improvement in subject knowledge

- consideration of different ways of helping pupils in PSHE/citizenship

- dealing with inappropriate/inadequate behaviour

Much can be done to help TAs to develop or improve if they are viewed as weak in certain aspects of their work. However, there may arise occasions when it becomes apparent that he or she may be unsuited to the work.

Such a conclusion is unlikely to arise purely as a result of a TA's work in PSHE and citizenship. It is more probable that it will be a whole-staff or senior management decision, taken as a result of a TA's work across the curriculum.

However, because of the more active approach of PSHE and citizenship, whereby the TA will encounter a wider variety of situations, evidence about unsuitability is likely to accumulate. PSHE and citizenship teachers might be advised to keep a log (discreetly) in such circumstances.

Developing some guidelines

It might be useful to consider some of the do's and don'ts which could apply to TAs working in the PSHE and citizenship fields.

Table 7.1 Guidelines for TAs in PSHE and citizenship

Don't force a pupil to take part in a discussion if he/she does not want to.

Do seek guidance from the teacher, and attempt to initiate a paired discussion with the pupil along the lines of the original discussion, but accept 'no' for an answer!

Don't force a pupil to become a reluctant member of a group.

Do talk to the pupil about why they do not want membership of a group and inform the teacher.

Don't take over the keyboard if a pupil is using IT to make an enquiry.

Do offer help and advice about what and where to search.

Don't sort the portfolio if you are helping a pupil to organise citizenship work.

Do suggest ways of organising, and encourage the pupil to consult other pupils who are organised and have good ideas.

Don't enter an argument between your pupil and another in lesson unless the atmosphere has become intimidating.

Do report the matter in full to the teacher and resolve a plan of action between you.

Appendices

Appendix 1	What Do We Really Think?
Appendix 2	INSET activity – SEN and Disability Act
Appendix 3	Keeping Strategies in Mind
Appendix 4.1	Activity – The Responsibility of Being a Dog Owner
Appendix 4.2	Key Words for Citizenship
Appendix 4.3(a)	Being a Good and Active Citizen
Appendix 4.3(b)	My Future
Appendix 4.4	Pupils on the Reception Desk – A Jobs Itinerary
Appendix 4.5	Lesson Ideas for Developing Empathy
Appendix 5.1	Differentiating Between Rights and Responsibilities
Appendix 5.2	A Questions Itinerary for the Story: 'Mugger, 5, Too Young To Be Prosecuted'
Appendix 5.3	Homework
Appendix 5.4	An Activity Sheet for 'London Children Share More Than 300 Languages'
Appendix 5.5	Activity Sheet for Creating a Fictional Teenager
Appendix 6.1	Secondary Case Studies
Appendix 6.2	Individual Education Plans
Appendix 6.3	Sample Care Action Plan
Appendix 7	Assisting TA Input in a Citizenship Lesson

What Do We Really Think?

Each member of the department should choose two of these statements and pin them on to the noticeboard for an overview of staff opinion. The person leading the session (Head of Department, SENCO, senior manager) should be ready to address any negative feedback and take forward the department in a positive approach.

If my own child had special needs, I would want her/him to be in a mainstream school mixing with all sorts of kids.

I want to be able to cater for pupils with SEN but feel that I don't have the expertise required.

Special needs kids in mainstream schools are all right up to a point, but I didn't sign up for dealing with the more severe problems – they should be in special schools.

It is the SENCO's responsibility to look out for these pupils with SEN – with help from support teachers.

Pupils with special needs should be catered for the same as any others. Teachers can't pick and choose the pupils they want to teach.

I need much more time to plan if pupils with SEN are going to be coming to my lessons.

Big schools are just not the right places for blind or deaf kids, or those in wheelchairs.

I would welcome more training on how to provide for pupils with SEN in citizenship and PSHE.

I have enough to do without worrying about kids who can't read or write.

If their behaviour distracts other pupils in any way, youngsters with SEN should be withdrawn from the class.

SEN and Disability Act 2001 (SENDA)

1 The SEN and Disability Act 2001 amends the Disability Discrimination Act 1995 to include schools' and LEAs' responsibility to provide for pupils and students with disabilities.

2 The definition of a disability in this Act is:

'someone who has a physical or mental impairment that has an effect on his or her ability to carry out normal day-to-day activities. The effect must be:

- substantial (that is more than minor or trivial); and
- long term (that is, has lasted or is likely to last for at least a year or for the rest of the life of the person affected); and
- adverse.'

Activity: List any pupils that you come across that would fall into this category.

3 The Act states that the responsible body for a school must take such steps as it is reasonable to take to ensure that disabled pupils and disabled prospective pupils are not placed at substantial disadvantage in comparison with those who are not disabled.

Activity: Give an example of something which might be considered 'a substantial disadvantage'.

4 The duty on the school to make reasonable adjustments is anticipatory. This means that a school should not wait until a disabled pupil seeks admission to consider what adjustments it might make generally to meet the needs of disabled pupils.

Activity: Think of two reasonable adjustments that could be made in your school/department.

5 The school has a duty to plan strategically for increasing access to the school education. This includes provision of information for pupils and parents (e.g. Braille or taped versions of brochures), improving the physical environment for disabled students, and increasing access to the curriculum by further differentiation.

Activity: Consider ways of increasing access to the school for a pupil requesting admission who has Down's Syndrome with low levels of literacy and a heart condition that affects strenuous physical activity.

6 Schools need to be proactive in seeking out information about a pupil's disability (by establishing good relationships with parents and carers, asking about disabilities during admission interviews, etc.) and ensuring that all staff who might come across the pupil are aware of the pupil's disability.

Activity: List the opportunities that occur in your school for staff to gain information about disabled students. How can these be improved on?

Keeping Strategies in Mind

Special Educational Need	Characteristics	Strategies
Attention Deficit Disorder – with or without hyperactivity	<ul><li>has difficulty following instructions and completing tasks</li><li>easily distracted by noise, movement of others, objects</li><li>can't stop talking, interrupts others, calls out</li><li>acts impulsively without thinking about the consequences</li></ul>	<ul><li>keep instructions simple – the one one sentence rule</li><li>make eye contact and use the pupil's name when speaking to him/her</li><li>sit the pupil away from obvious distractions</li><li>provide clear routines and rules, rehearse them regularly</li></ul>
Autistic Spectrum Disorder	<ul><li>may experience high levels of stress and anxiety when routines are changed</li><li>may have a literal understanding of language</li><li>more often interested in objects than people</li><li>may be sensitive to light, sound, touch or smell</li></ul>	<ul><li>give a timetable for each day</li><li>warn the pupil about changes to usual routine</li><li>avoid using too much eye contact as it can cause distress</li><li>use simple clear language, avoid using metaphor, sarcasm</li></ul>
Down's Syndrome	<ul><li>takes longer to learn and consolidate new skills</li><li>limited concentration</li><li>has difficulties with thinking, reasoning, sequencing</li><li>has better social than academic skills</li><li>may have some sight, hearing, respiratory and heart problems</li></ul>	<ul><li>use simple, familiar language</li><li>give time for information to be processed</li><li>break lesson up into a series of shorter, varied tasks</li><li>accept a variety of ways of recording work, drawings, diagrams, photos, video</li></ul>

| Hearing Impairment | Hearing in one ear only – May have a monoaural loss | • check on the best seating position
• check that the pupil can see your face for expressions and lip reading
• indicate where a pupil is speaking from during class discussion, only allow one speaker at a time |
| Dyscalculia | • has a discrepancy between development level and general ability in maths
• has difficulty counting by rote
• misses out or reverses numbers
• has difficulty with directions, left and right
• losing track of turns in games, dance | • provide visual aids, number lines, lists of rules, formulae, words
• encourage working out on paper
• provide practical objects to aid learning |

Instructions for activity

This activity should only take about ten minutes but can be used for additional discussion on strategies, concentrating on the easy ones to implement or the ones already being used.

1 Photocopy onto paper or card.
2 Cut the first column off the sheet.
3 Cut out the remaining boxes.
4 Either keep the two sets of boxes separate, first matching the characteristics then the strategies, or use all together.

Alternative activity: make the boxes bigger with room for additional strategies, or remove a couple of the strategies so staff can add any they have used or can identify.

The Responsibility of Being a Dog Owner

Everyone has the right to own a dog
BUT
The court can take away the dog if the owner does not show RESPONSIBILITY

Name four responsibilities towards the dog.

1.

2.

3.

4.

Name four responsibilities towards the community.

1.

2.

3.

4.

Tom is a responsible dog owner. Describe him.

Leah is not a responsible dog owner. Describe her.

Key words for Citizenship

Social
Legal
Human rights
Responsibilities
Society
Community
Justice system
Diversity
National
Ethnic
Central government

Local government
Public services
Parliament
Elections
Voting
Voluntary
Conflict
Conflict resolution
Media
Global
Political

Economic
Environment(al)
Moral
Opinion
Debate
Discussion
Justify
Reflect
Criminal
Civil

(a) Year 7 lesson: Being a Good and Active Citizen

Introduction

Pupils are organised into groups of fives and sixes and encouraged to share their homework projects on 'What kind of citizen am I?' (featuring a passport size photo plus five sentences using key words) (10 minutes)

Development

1 Pupils asked individually to make lists of jobs/duties undertaken at primary school, (not fewer than two or more than four). (10 minutes)

2 Pupils return to small groups and, after citing one thing they liked and one thing they disliked about primary school, they compare jobs they did. (10 minutes)

3 The teacher appoints group leaders and each group makes a list of the best ten jobs undertaken by group members. (10 minutes)

4 Whole-class discussion. Teacher gives examples of 'active citizenship' in wider society (e.g. people who run charity shops), and seeks examples from pupils of people who 'do' things that help society. (10 minutes)

Plenary

Teacher hands out a sheet 'Good and active citizens' which amounts to a summary of the lesson. On one side of the sheet is 'Duties undertaken at primary school'; on the other is 'Roles undertaken by citizens'. (This is to be completed for homework.)

(b) Year 9 lesson: My Future

Introduction

In the previous week, the class is given an A4 sheet with a spider diagram. In the spider's body is the question: 'What's important to me?' Twelve legs radiate outwards, and the teacher explains that twelve is the maximum number of responses and four the minimum. It is carefully explained that one can choose issues, events, people and hobbies. The teacher uses some disclosure to exemplify the exercise. Pupils complete sheet and hand in.

Development

1   Teacher hands back the previous week's sheets which have been annotated with questions and positive comments only. Allows time for study. (5 minutes)

2   Three pre-selected pupils (two if time is limited) are now briefly interviewed by the teacher at the front of the class. Once each interview is over, members of the class can ask questions. (Up to 20 minutes)

3   (Optional if limited time is available.) Class is paired up so each pupil can be interviewed about their response. Sheet is then placed in file/workbook. (10 minutes)

4   Each pupil is given a sheet headed 'My future'. On this they must make four statements:

   (a) My ambition for the future

   (b) The most positive thing that ever happened to me

   (c) What I hope to be doing when I am 30

   (d) What I hope people will say about me after I die (15 minutes)

Conclusion/Plenary

Class is split into groups of three and/or four and each group member's sheet is reviewed by the whole group.
   The questioning model is:

   (1) Are the statements sincere?

   (2) Are they realistic?

   (3) What values do the statements show (i.e. what matters most)?

This model is carefully explained by the teacher and the groups are carefully constructed.

Pupils on the Reception Desk – A Jobs Itinerary

1 Meeting visitors to the school and acting as liaison between them and the school office. Showing visitors to meeting rooms.

2 Basic photocopying tasks.

3 Repairing, amending, taking down wall displays.

4 Within-school courier service.

5 Collecting spare paper from rooms for recycling.

6 Managing the school's own recycling initiative (paper, glass, plastic, ribbons and cartridges, etc.).

7 Tidying up of class registers (logging sick notes, mending torn pages, etc.).

8 Stapling booklets.

9 Contributing to/researching for the school newsletter.

10 Maintaining a pupils-only message board.

Lesson Ideas for Developing Empathy

Citizenship is the most appropriate subject for developing awareness of the issues faced by pupils with SEN.

1 Pupils could be equipped with thick gardening gloves and asked to complete delicate handling tasks in order to give them an idea of how dyspraxia affects some pupils.

2 Pupils could be asked to try out mirror-writing to experience how difficult the task of writing is for some pupils (mirror is placed at right angles to the paper and the pupil copies a set piece of writing, using only the mirror image as his/her guide).

3 Blindfolded pupils are led on a set journey across the school and provided with a guide.

4 For half a day on the school timetable, right-handed pupils are to do everything with their left hand.

5 The teacher introduces to the class the idea that recent scientfic research has shown that blue-eyed pupils are more intelligent than pupils with any other colour eyes (he/she must keep perfectly serious). A task is then given out appropriate to the subject, and the teacher informs the class that she is going to test the research by giving blue-eyed pupils a harder version of the same work. After, say, 30 minutes, the teacher collects the work in and admits the exercise was a 'con'. Pupils discuss their feelings.

6 A small group of pupils wear thick wads of cottonwool in their ears for a part of a lesson. Sufficient time is left at the end of the lesson for a discussion about how it affected them, etc.

7 The teacher can construct a lesson whereby he/she is distinctly more friendly and helpful towards one gender than the other, even to the point of rudeness and exclusion. Allow sufficient time at the end of the lesson to discuss feelings, and how this might relate to pupils who are ostracised by others.

Differentiating Between Rights and Responsibilities

Decide whether the descriptions below belong under the 'rights' or 'responsibilities' label:

To obey the law 	**To get a fair trial if you are charged with a criminal offence** 
Free speech 	**To drive a motor car when you are aged 18** 
To pay taxes 	**To vote at an election** 

Not to drop litter	To receive an education
	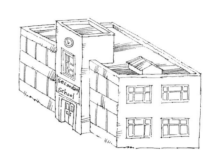
To be granted a British passport	**Not to make a noise which disturbs neighbours**

To keep a household pet	To pay for a TV licence

A Questions Itinerary for the Story: 'Mugger, 5, Too Young To Be Prosecuted'

1   Why do you think these children are not bothered about what they have done or what might happen? What needs to be done to improve their situation?

2   Should the parents of the five-year-old be prosecuted by the police? If not, why not? If so, what would be the point? If they were taken to court, how should they be punished?

3   Suppose the boys had been ten years older than they were, should the Johnson family still have got involved? What things should someone consider when they decide to 'have a go' at a criminal?

4   Do you think ten years old is the right age to be held responsible for a crime? What rights would you have if the police wanted to question you about an incident?

With thanks to 'Including Special Children' *for the use of this activity sheet (Issue 149, September 2002)*

(Taking the strain out of) Homework

Twenty worthwhile citizenship/PSHE homework activities which suit pupils with SEN and do not involve copious writing and marking!

1   Ask pupils to find an issue in a national paper and bring it to school for discussion. (They should be prepared to outline the argument presented.)

2   Give pupils a list of five or more key citizenship words to learn the spellings and/or meanings.

3   Read the letters page of the local newspaper and ask pupils to select the letters with which they (a) most agree (b) most disagree.

4   Use local or national newspapers to make a news collage (similar to the backdrop in the TV show *Have I Got News For You*)

5   Present the class with a news story on a contentious issue. Ask them to create three questions they would like to ask the journalist.

6   Ask pupils to do Internet research on Google or Lycos on a specified topic and print out the results.

7   Conflict resolution. Focus on a conflict and ask pupils to work in pairs to come up with a resolution (explain the conflict to ensure everyone has the same understanding).

8   Interview a parent about an issue. (Ask pupils to take notes that they can present in class later.)

9   Words in a sentence. Pick (say) three new words which arise in a lesson and ask pupils to create a sentence featuring each word.

10 Personal collage. On an A4 sheet, ask pupils to make a pictorial representation of their identity. (Encourage use of digital camera, etc.)

11 With a friend make up a circle game (that the class can play).

12 Make a collage of a particular emotion (e.g. fear, happiness, worry).

13 Keep an eating diary for one week (follow with a lesson on healthy eating).

14 Consider the school and grounds so that you can say in a later discussion where are the safest and least safe places for younger pupils.

15 Consider your journey home from school. Where are the main accident black spots?

16 Watch the TV news and make a list of all the items in running order. (The teacher can then pin up the lists on a temporary noticeboard.)

17 Imagine the school had its own news programme. Write a news story (40 words maximum?) which you think could be included (to be presented in class).

18 Use the Internet to find out all you can about an environmental issue. Decide where you stand on it.

19 Do one good deed for someone else and talk about it in class next lesson.

20 Give pupils a list of ten jobs and ask them to decide which is the most and least important (compare lists in class).

An Activity Sheet for 'London Children Share More Than 300 Languages'

1   Try and think of a language to go with the following letters of the alphabet:

B	C	F
G	L	N
P	R	S
T	W	

2   'A problem is an opportunity in disguise.' Each person in the group thinks of a problem they have at school or at home, and considers how it could be a chance to do something differently.

3   Think of six different kinds of jobs London can offer because people who live there speak so many different languages, for example charity organisers for different countries.

4   Think of six different problems a school might have if its pupils speak many different languages.

Activity Sheet for Creating a Fictional Teenager

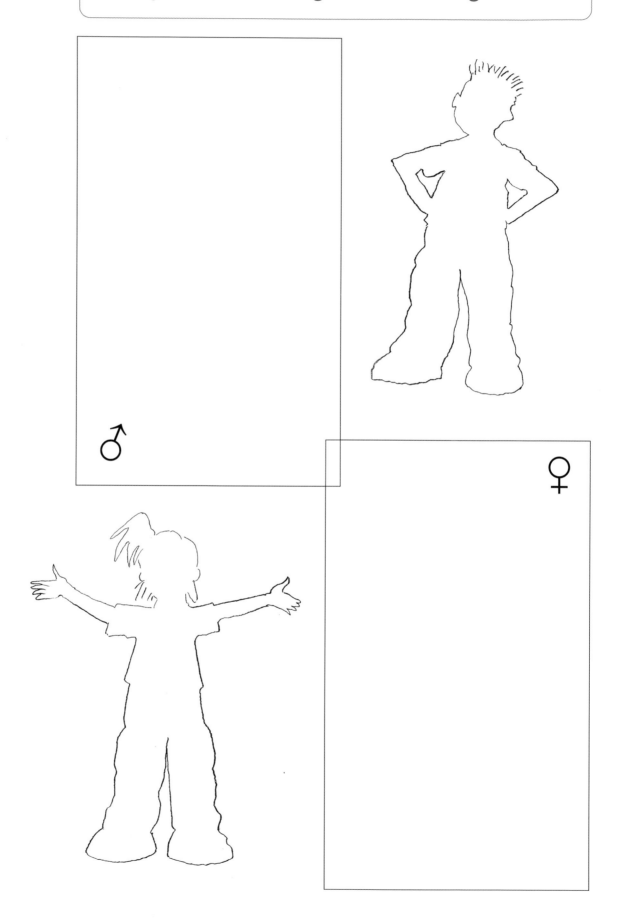

Secondary Case Studies

Ashraf – Year 8. Citizenship

Within the Key Stage 3 'knowledge, skills and understanding', pupils should be taught about 'the electoral system and the importance of voting'. (60 mins)

Ashraf is working in a mixed ability class for citizenship. He has cerebral palsy and severe learning difficulties and uses a wheelchair to move between lessons and a Kay walker for moving around the classroom. He can be reluctant to speak in class, but the regular use of discussion and pupil interaction means that Ashraf is as sociable in this lesson as any. He uses a laptop computer for all writing tasks.

Ashraf is working at P7 of the P scales for PSHE/citizenship:

P7 Pupils communicate feelings and ideas in simple phrases. They move, with support, to new activities which are either directed or self-chosen. They make purposeful relationships with others in group activities and attempt to negotiate them with a variety of situations. They judge right and wrong on the basis of the consequences of their actions. They show some consideration of the needs and feelings of other people and other living things.

Support

Ashraf has a 1-1 Teaching Assistant because of his learning and personal needs. Ashraf's teacher and his TA planned the unit of work together to agree the principal objectives in a double lesson package which would communicate a lot of information to pupils. This lesson was targeted because it met an important objective in Ashraf's IEP and the TA has ensured that Ashraf has his own version of certain resources.

Background

In this two-lesson package, the first lesson of the previous week had introduced to the pupils the ideas of political parties and voting. The class was split into three groups – New Labour, Conservative and Liberal Democrat – and each group was given a theme colour and a symbol. They were then given a policy line about the school's extensive playing fields: New Labour would sell off half for building development and use the money to develop school facilities; Conservatives would sell most of the grounds for hi-tech industry to boost the town's employment openings; and the Liberal Democrats (Ashraf's group) wish to preserve the grounds in keeping with their environmental concerns. Ashraf's TA interpreted all that was going on and he took part in electing a group leader as the speaker for the following week.

Lesson 2 of the unit: party speeches and the vote

Objectives

Pupils will learn:

- to listen to a speaker and ask questions to clarify and to undermine

- how to vote and organise the count

Ashraf's objectives for this lesson

Ashraf will learn:

- to understand that leaders explain their actions and are then assessed by those they lead

- to learn how voting occurs (through his own involvement)

IEP target addressed in this lesson

Social & communication skills: making purposeful relationships in group activities.

Target vocabulary for this lesson: voting, election.

Activities

1 Ashraf listens to the teacher recounting last week's lesson. His TA reinforces the teacher's words by placing the theme colours and symbols before Ashraf, reminding him that he is in the Liberal Democrat group. (10 minutes)

2 Each speaker has a maximum four minutes, followed by three questions from the audience (indicated by hands-up). The TA takes care to point out the mechanism at work here. Having seen the speeches in advance, the TA outlines the basic ideas to Ashraf in the very simplest of forms. (20 minutes)

3 Pupils queue to receive voting forms which Ashraf hands to them as the TA ticks off each pupil's name on the class list. Ashraf was prepared for this by discussion with his TA during registration. Finally, Ashraf is given his own voting form. (10 minutes)

4 The teacher is using his stockroom as an election booth. Using an OHP, he explains that the voter puts an X against the candidate they support, illustrating the ways in which a vote can be spoiled. Each pupil is called alphabetically to vote (beginning with A for Ashraf) and posts their vote in a specially made box. (Ashraf helped to make this in design and technology.) (10 minutes)

5 While the teacher sums up the speeches and processes in the plenary, Ashraf and his TA count the vote. (Ashraf puts them in three piles and counts with the TA supervising the count.) (10 minutes)

6 Ashraf announces the result to the class where there is much cheering and booing at the result! The TA has arranged a 10-minute debriefing session afterwards with Ashraf so that he can understand the significance of the vote and that the class reaction was not aimed at him! (10 minutes)

TA Liaison Sheet

To Ashraf's TA

1 Please explain the idea of voting to Ashraf. These are the terms I would like him to understand:

Voting slip   Ballot box   Election   Majority

2 Go over the colour themes and symbols for each party.

3 If 1 is very attentive and 5 is almost no attention, how would you rate Ashraf as a listener to the speakers?

(Make sure you see the speeches in advance so that you can go over them with Ashraf)

4 Let Ashraf vote in advance (in the ballot box he helped to make in technology).

5 When you start the count, introduce the idea of counting the votes in three separate piles.

6 Give Ashraf all the help he needs when announcing the result of the vote.

7 Please make time for a 10-minute debrief.

Ryan – Year 11. Citizenship

Key Stage 4 Citizenship: Developing skills of participation and responsible action – pupils should be taught to negotiate, decide and take part responsibly in school and community-based activities. (Double lesson of two x 50 minutes)

Ryan has profound and multiple learning difficulties and uses a wheelchair for all his time in school. He has always attended mainstream schools and enjoys the company of boys of his own age. He enjoys watching sport, particularly football, and his dad has taken him to support Sheffield United in the special viewing area on a number of occasions.

Ryan communicates by eye pointing and smiling and becomes animated whenever he is going anywhere out of the ordinary.

Ryan is working at level P2 (ii) of the P scales in PSHE/citizenship:

P 2 (ii) Pupils begin to be proactive in their interactions. They communicate consistent preferences and affective responses. They recognise familiar people, events and objects. They perform actions, often by trial and improvement, and they remember learned responses over short periods of time. They cooperate with shared exploration and supported participation.

Support

Ryan has two teaching assistants, Geoff and Shefali, who share his support across the week. Geoff was appointed when one of the previous TAs retired. Having a man to support him has given a boost to Ryan's self-image. Geoff is a football fan too, although he supports Sheffield Wednesday and this makes for some gentle teasing between him and Ryan. Geoff is a keen swimmer and is seen as the natural choice for this lesson within a visit to the local swimming pool.

Background

Ryan enjoys sitting in a specially adapted bath he has at home, although it is quite a task to get him into the water. He has never bathed in a communal facility.

Throughout Years 10 and 11, the teacher for PSHE and citizenship has been concentrating on access to local amenities. She has assessed this as a priority area since there is a recent local history of school leavers getting in trouble and blaming a lack of things to do as a reason. When she read in the local paper that the town swimming pool was to undergo a refurbishment, she thought it was too good an opportunity to miss.

After a preliminary visit to the site manager, she was delighted to learn that it was not too late to involve the school in planning for the pool's refurbishment. Pupils will be bussed to the pool for a question and answer session which will include full access to a 3-D model of the intended development.

The pupils will be allowed to have a 30-minute session in the present pool before the interview session.

Class objectives
The pupils will learn:

- how to contribute to local democracy through a considered response to change

- how planning occurs in order to improve local facilities

Ryan's objectives for the lesson at P2 (ii)
Ryan will learn:

- to recognise that people's ideas can alter and improve things

IEP target addressed in this lesson
Social & Communication skills: recognising that he is part of a teenage group with shared concerns.

Target vocabulary: swimming pool, plan, model.

Activities

1   Although Ryan is taken in the school minibus (which has wheelchair access), a number of the class accompany him while the rest take a hire bus. Geoff accompanies Ryan and during the journey he goes over the purpose of the lesson. (15 minutes)

2   The class are allowed a 30-minute bathing session and Geoff takes Ryan (in his wheelchair) into the boys' changing room so that he can see the changing system (lockers, keys, etc.) and facilities in action. Geoff talks him through while wheeling him around the area.

3   Geoff wheels Ryan into the main pool area and, after a chance to watch his friends in the water, takes him to the infant pool. When the refurbishment occurs, a special area is to be designated for wheelchair users at this end of the pool. Geoff explains this. (35 minutes)

4   While pupils are changing into their school clothes, Geoff takes Ryan into the area set aside for the meeting with the site manager. He shows Ryan the plan (on the wall) of the redeveloped swimming pool and then moves on to the table-mounted 3-D model. By the time pupils gather in the room, Ryan is parked and ready for the session. (10 minutes)

5   Following an explanation of the refurbishment (with reference to the model) pupils are allowed to ask questions of the site manager. They are then given slips of paper and each one is invited to suggest an idea in writing for the re-developed amenity. Ryan also takes part in this with Geoff writing down the idea which the two of them agree. (25 minutes)

6   The same arrangements for returning to school as for the outward journey.

Specimen letter home (For Ryan's parents)

Dear

In today's citizenship lesson, Ryan visited the swimming pool. The school is advising the authorities about the amenities young people would prefer when the pool is refurbished and we thought this would be a good experience for Ryan.

He thoroughly enjoyed the journey to and from the pool. His Teaching Assistant, Geoff, was impressed that Ryan understood both the point of the exercise and how the changing facilities, etc. were used.

Through Geoff, Ryan submitted a question:

Will there be a pool I can sit in?

I am pleased to say his request is being given serious consideration.

Yours sincerely,

Sarah – Year 7. Citizenship

Sarah transferred from a small primary school three months ago. She has a diagnosis of Asperger's Syndrome but her academic achievement so far has been below the average for her age. Sarah had behavioural difficulties at primary school, but these have not surfaced since the transfer to secondary. Rather, she has been quiet, withdrawn and anxious, drifting away from the few friends she had in her previous school. Sarah appears to be articulate, but her comprehension of both written and spoken English is poor.

Support

She has five hours support time on her statement of special educational needs. The school uses these hours flexibly to give her support when it is most needed. In the first term she had support in PHSE and citizenship on those occasions her teacher requested it (usually when working in small groups as a hedge against Sarah isolating herself). This was reasonably successful except for one week when the group did some turn-taking and Sarah was unable to cope with the limelight. Her TA sat with her quietly in a corner when this happened.

All the staff had an INSET on Autistic Spectrum Disorders before Sarah transferred. The teacher makes sure homework tasks are understood and written down before Sarah leaves the lesson.

Background

Having spent the first term on PSHE issues like eating and lifestyle choices, the course now goes on to define citizenship by encouraging pupils to look at themselves and their own lives as a starting point.

The first week was spent considering 'What kind of citizen am I?' with Sarah being asked to come up with five key words that mark out her identity in a positive way. Her choices were – girl, English, mouse, scarf, car.

For homework, pupils were asked to find a small photo and beneath it write five short sentences providing a context for each word.

Sarah needed a lot of TA help, but it emerged that 'mouse' was her pet, the family recently had a new car and she wanted to keep wearing her scarf because it was cold.

Now the teacher wishes to take the lesson forward by getting pupils to consider how they contribute to society.

Class objective
Pupils will:

● reflect on ways in which pupils are already citizens, particularly through participation in both school and community

Sarah's IEP targets addressed in this lesson

Communication & Social Skills: Sarah will co-operate in small group work by joining in.

Target vocabulary: citizen, active, cooperate.

Activities

1 All pupils are encouraged to make a list of how they were involved in the life of their primary school (jobs, duties, chores, etc.). Not fewer than two or more than four items to be in the list. Sarah lists 'reading my book' and 'cleaning up after packed lunch'. At this point her TA does not interfere. (10 minutes)

2 Pupils now put into groups of fives or sixes and asked to discuss their primary schools. Everyone in the group is to come up with one aspect of life at primary school they liked and one they disliked (turn-talking in alphabetical order). If there is time, group to compare the differences between schools. Sarah's TA contributes first (from her own schooldays so that Sarah will have a model). Sarah says she hated it when it rained and liked watering the plants (her TA realises that an opportunity has been missed for her jobs list and so he suggests it to Sarah). (15 minutes)

3 The teacher appoints group leaders and asks them to collect a list of the best ten jobs undertaken by group members at primary school. Sarah's TA comes under pressure to be the group secretary. This would have its advantages, but she knows that 'taking your own responsibility' is the theme of the next lesson and she doesn't want to cut across this. The group is very good with Sarah and she is pleased when her watering the flowers is included on the group list and is read out by the teacher in the plenary. (20 minutes)

4 The teacher explains that people who take part are known as 'active citizens' and asks for examples of active citizenship in wider society. Sarah's TA quietly encourages her to come up with an example, but she seems very tired and this is something that can be followed up when she reviews her homework with her. (10 minutes)

5 Teacher hands out a sheet 'Good and active citizens' which amounts to a summary of the lesson – duties undertaken at primary school and roles undertaken voluntarily by adult citizens. Sarah's TA knows she will have to do this with her at school, but rather than go through the 'answers' she will let Sarah quiz her classmates. (5 minutes)

Charlene – Year 10. Citizenship and PSHE

Citizenship: Developing skills of participation and responsible action – negotiate, decide and take part responsibly in school and community-based activities.

Charlene is in Year 10. She has Williams Syndrome and severe learning difficulties. Her expressive language is very good but her understanding of language and her short-term memory skills are very delayed. Charlene is a very sociable person with an infectious giggle. She is easily upset by any conflict or aggression – real or perceived. She thoroughly enjoys copy writing and is a compulsive colourer. Possesses basic IT skills.

Charlene's performance level can vary alarmingly, but she has been assessed at approximately level six of the P scales.

P6. Pupils respond to others in group situations, playing or working in a small group cooperatively. They carry out routine activities in a familiar context and show an awareness of the results of their own actions. They may show concern for others, and sympathy for others in distress, and offer comfort.

Support

Charlene has ten hours' support on her statement of special educational needs. The school uses these hours flexibly to target support where Charlene most needs it. PSHE/citizenship uses support for approximately one lesson per fortnight. Throughout her time at the school Charlene has been supported by a peer buddy system. This suits her gregarious personality and has led to her being relatively mature and independent.

Background

PSHE and citizenship is taught in small mixed-ability groups from Year 7 (approximately 20 to 23 in number) and the department has a tradition of using group work creatively to provide support for problem pupils.

Academically able pupils have been brought up to accept that, as this is not a lesson which needs to meet exam requirements, working as a team and helping others are important goals. Charlene was the beneficiary of this approach in the peer buddy system.

The pupils have been looking at the voluntary sector in class and four weeks ago were visited by an impressive speaker from the charity Shelter. Because the town has a real problem with homeless people, two Year 10 PSHE/citizenship groups have decided to run a Saturday morning jumble sale to raise funds for Shelter. This lesson will determine the organisation of the day.

Objectives for this lesson

Pupils will:

- consider every aspect of organisation required for the jumble sale
- allocate duties accordingly

119

Objectives for Charlene

Charlene will:

- obtain some understanding of how a community event is organised

- define her own role on the day itself

IEP target addressed in this lesson

Social & Communication Skills: to show commitment to a particular task and see it through to conclusion.

Activities

Owing to the special nature of the project Charlene's group have undertaken, they have been granted a full afternoon off timetable to prepare:

1 One female member of the group has already been involved in Charlene's peer buddy programme. She has been in conversation with Charlene's TA in preparation for this lesson.

2 Between Charlene and her partner, they agree upon six shops in the vicinity of school in which they could stick a poster advertising the jumble sale.

3 They take it in turns to phone each establishment to ask whether they will agree to display a poster. The able pupil makes the model phone call and helps Charlene to make notes so that she can make the last two of the six phone calls.

4 The pair design a poster on the computer using a template from Microsoft Publisher or similar. They are overseen by Charlene's TA who makes sure that Charlene gets a reasonable input into the design of the poster.

5 Charlene helps with the posting/delivery of the posters.

TA liaison sheet

To Charlene's TA

1 I understand you have chosen Stella W to partner Charlene for this activity – Please establish with her:

- appropriate basis for choosing shops

- issues to cover in phone calls to shops

2 Be prepared to walk round the local area looking at shops with them.

3 Listen in on their telephone calling and make sure it's appropriate.

4 Before they design the poster on computer, encourage them to do a pen and paper 'dummy'.

5 Arrange the poster delivery.

Matthew – Year 9. Citizenship/PSHE

Citizenship – knowledge and understanding – pupils should be taught 'the legal and human rights underpinning society'.

Matthew is a very passive boy. He has no curiosity, no strong likes or dislikes. One teacher said, 'He's the sort of boy who says yes to everything to avoid further discussion but I sometimes wonder if he understands anything.'

Now in Year 9, he is quite a loner. He knows all the pupils and does not feel uncomfortable with them but is always on the margins. Often in class he sits and does nothing, just stares into space. He is no trouble and indeed if there is any kind of conflict, he absents himself or ignores it. No one knows very much about him as he never volunteers any information.

He does every piece of work as quickly as possible to get it over with. His work is messy and there is no substance to anything he does which makes it hard for teachers to suggest a way forward, or indeed to find anything to praise. Matthew looks a bit grubby and is usually untidy. He can be quite clumsy and loses things regularly but does not bother to look for them. He does less than the minimum.

He has problems with most humanities subjects because he has no empathy and no real sense of what is required. When the class did a museum visit, he was completely unmoved. To him it was just another building and he could not really link it with the work the class had done in history.

Support

The school has identified Matthew on the autistic spectrum and has drawn up an IEP accordingly, but his statementing is only two years old. Because his autism is only mild, he has been allocated just five hours a week of TA time, all of which is spoken for in English, maths and science. However, there is some concern that Matthew shows minimal responsibility for his actions and this has shown itself in anti-social behaviour in the English lesson. After a conversation between the English and PSHE/citizenship teachers, it has been agreed to transfer the TA time to the latter for one week.

Matthew's TA is an experienced lady who knows Matthew's mother quite well and there is a concern that she freely passes on information to the home which might not be in anyone's interests.

Background

Matthew has displayed no more involvement with this unit of citizenship work than with any other. The teacher's approach has been to use lots of true stories from the press as discussion points, but Matthew is reluctant to engage with other members of the class and, in any case, seems to have a great reluctance to speak out his thoughts in class.

A worrying recent development has been a flare-up between Matthew and two other Year 9 boys. These two boys have already 'set about' Matthew on the way home and recently mother came up to school to sort out a strategy to keep Matthew out of harm. A part of the strategy involves mum picking Matthew up by car after school. One unfortunate outcome of the grouping is that one of the two boys concerned is in this class with Matthew.

Lesson 2 of the unit: the law and under age youngsters

Objectives
Pupils will:

- think about the age of criminal responsibility

- consider the causes of crime

Target vocabulary: criminal responsibility.

Matthew's objectives for this lesson
Matthew will:

- contribute to a group discussion

- show concern for others

IEP target addressed in this lesson
Social & Communication skills: to become involved in a discussion and relate to at least one other pupil in the class.

Activities

1 Plenary session. Class arrive and sit in a circle. Teacher writes term 'Criminal responsibility' on the board. She asks the class how many situations they can think of in which a person commits a crime but cannot then be considered responsible. She then gives the class two minutes' thinking time to consult neighbours (Matthew's TA draws in Matthew and two others around him to focus on the question). Answers are eventually gleaned which bring out sanity, provocation and age. (10 minutes)

2 Teacher distributes a press story 'Mugger, 5, is too young to be prosecuted'. This is about two boys aged five and nine who stole a pensioner's handbag. She uses readers from around the class (including Matthew) with no more than three sentences each. After the reading the teacher summarises the story in a factual, non-emotional way so that everyone understands the issues. (10 minutes)

3 The teacher announces groups of four and five which she has carefully prepared so that genders are mixed and two academically able pupils are in each group. Areas on the classroom are assigned to each group and pupils have to move to that area. The teacher has made it clear that group

membership on this occasion is non-negotiable. (The TA has been instructed to work generally, but to keep the closest eye on Matthew's group.) (5 minutes)

4   The story has been divided into five discussion topics. Matthew's group have been given:

Should the five-year-old's parents be prosecuted instead of him? If not, why not? If so, what would that achieve? What might be an appropriate way of treating the parents?

The group votes for a leader and a secretary (which they are used to doing). Everyone must make comment which the secretary records in note form to be read out by the speaker at the end of the lesson. Majority opinions are sounded out. (20 minutes)

5   Plenary. The class returns to the circle format and group leaders read out their report for general listening and comment. (15 minutes)

Monitoring sheet

Matthew

How did Matthew settle?

1   in the circle

2   in a small group

Which pupils did Matthew relate (talk) to?

On a scale of 1 (very involved) to 5 (totally uninterested), how did you rate Matthew today? (Please explain your mark.)

Jenny – Year 7. PSHE/citizenship

Key Stage 3 – PSHE guidelines:

- expressing positive qualities about themselves and others

- recognising feelings in different situations and what might cause them, and managing them

- knowing personal likes and dislikes

- expressing feelings in different ways and understanding their impact on others

Jenny is in Year 7 and has Down's Syndrome. She is a very confident child who has been cherished and encouraged by her mother and older brothers and sisters. She is very assertive and is more than capable of dealing with spiteful comments: 'I don't like it when you call me names. You're cruel and I hate you.' But this assertiveness can lead to obstinacy. She is prone to telling teachers that they are wrong.

She has average reading and writing skills, but her work tends to be unimaginative and pedestrian. Apart from getting on well with the biology teacher, she finds science hard-going. Because she's started putting on weight, she tries to avoid PE by getting mum to write notes. In truth, she is energetic and active with a good singing voice and an enjoyment of dancing.

At primary school, she was treated as someone special and got invited to everyone's birthday party. Teachers and helpers frequently praised her and made her feel special. In secondary school, everything has changed. Her old primary school friends have made new friendships and she feels excluded and rejected. She is also struck by how glamorous some of the older girls look and this has made her more self-conscious. Jenny is achieving level 2 in English which is the best guide to her performance in PSHE/citizenship.

Support

Jenny has ten hours a week and the school has managed to carry over the TA who supported her in the primary school, Sonia. Having been with her since age six, Sonia has a particularly valuable context for working with Jenny. Because the school is targeting Jenny's social and emotional development in Year 7, PSHE has been seen as one of the lessons in which she will receive regular support.

Background

This is the first of a group of lessons which will clearly impact very directly on Jenny's life. Her TA has been made well aware of this and realises that the classroom situation calls for her to focus not just on Jenny's behaviour, but also that of her classmates towards her (particularly peers from her primary school).

This lesson on 'body language' could equally well have been taught at KS2, but it is the first of a set of four which will lead on into TV-assisted learning, role play, etc. so it is important that Jenny identifies with the topic.

Class objectives
Pupils will:

- explore non-verbal communication

- develop a vocabulary for expressing emotions

Jenny's objectives
Jenny will:

- begin to understand how to cope with different emotions

IEP target addressed in this lesson
Social & Communication skills: expressing her emotions with language rather than actions.

Target vocabulary for this lesson: emotion.

Activities

1   Teacher introduces topic to pupils in circle by referring to animal communication, particularly dogs and cats (e.g. how do dogs show pleasure?) Examples are gleaned after children are given a chance to discuss with 'neighbours'. Teacher introduces term 'body language'. (10 minutes)

2   Ask question: Do you think humans can communicate in this way? Class are divided into six numbered groups (TA and teacher have 'fixed' Jenny's group so that three of her ex-primary peers are in it). (5 minutes)

3   It is explained that pupils are going to look closely at human 'body language' and try to work out what each of six characters are feeling. Photocopiable sheet given out and each pupil individually decides what each character is thinking and shares with rest of group. (15 minutes)

4   In their books, pupils try to write two or three words associated with each character (they are: misery, joy, envy, anger, anxiety, frustration). TA and teacher move round groups helping. (5 minutes)

5   Teacher has pinned six sheets of flipchart paper around wall and pupils, for relevant number, chart their words. Teacher reviews and publicly notes there is overlap and confusion (makes point that sometimes body language is tricky to interpret). (10 minutes)

6   Teacher asks each group to discuss one way in which the character that they have been given might help him/herself to manage the feeling. A volunteer from each group is to write the idea at the bottom of the sheet. (TA is targeting Jenny's group at this point and helping to manage Jenny's contribution.) Groups then visit each other's poster. (10 minutes)

7 Teacher discusses the idea of 'managing emotions' with the whole class in a circle. They are also asked to consider how they can apply this lesson to their own lives. (5 minutes)

Monitoring sheet

Jenny

Understanding:

On a scale of 1 (fully understands) to 5 (minimal comprehension), how did you rate Jenny today? (Please explain your mark.)

Emotions:

Which emotions do you think she identified?

Language:

What emotional vocabulary did she use? *(Explanation about emotional vocabulary will have been given earlier.)*

Megan – Year 10. PSHE/citizenship

Nicknamed 'Miss Angry', everyone knows when Megan is around! She is very outgoing, loud and tough. No one feels sorry for her – they wouldn't dare. Megan has spina bifida and needs a wheelchair and personal care as well as educational support. She has upset a number of the less experienced TAs who find her a real pain. Some of the teachers like her because she is sparky. If she likes a subject she works hard – or at least she did until this year.

Megan has to be up very early so that she can be ready for school before the bus comes at 7.50 a.m. She lives out of town and is one of the first to be picked up and one of the last to be dropped off. This gives her a longer school day than most of her classmates. Obviously, tiredness can be a real problem.

Now she's 15 she has started to work towards her GCSEs and has the potential to get several A to Cs, particularly in maths and sciences. She is intelligent but is in danger of becoming disaffected because everything is so much harder for her than most pupils. Recently she lost her temper with a teacher, made cruel remarks to a sensitive child and turned her wheelchair round so she sat with her back to a supply teacher. She has done no homework for the last few weeks saying that she doesn't see the point as 'no one takes a crip seriously'.

Support

Jill, who is a very experienced TA, has been providing Megan's support since she arrived at secondary school. Jill is a quiet, resolute character who can take all that Megan 'throws' at her and continue to deal with her in a rational, calm way. She works with Megan all day, but gets one hour's respite at lunchtime when a midday supervisor takes over. Break and lunchtime have become a problem recently as Megan has become so offensive that many of her friends and acquaintances no longer want to share her company.

Background

In many ways Megan exemplifies this group. Mr Barrington, who teaches them, often sees them as a bunch of misfits. In all his 20 years' experience he has rarely seen a class with such poor chemistry. Consequently, he has asked the head of PSHE for permission to temporarily suspend the syllabus and work on the group's development skills. It occurs to him that Megan is an island of difficulty in a stormy sea, but he is determined to make progress. There is an energy about the class and if they can achieve some degree of fusion, then he feels they could 'take off'.

In preparation for this lesson, Jill spent some time during registration explaining to Megan that her social skills were causing concern. Megan is well aware of her IEP and Jill explains that she really needs to work on the particular target mentioned below. Megan's response is muted, but at least she does not 'kick off'.

Class objectives
Pupils will:

- become aware of how people support one another in groups

- develop thinking skills

Megan's objective
Megan will:

- contribute as a member of a team

IEP target addressed in this lesson
Social and communication skills: taking the lead in making purposeful relationships with others.

Activities

1   Mr Barrington opens with a plenary about 'working together'. He asks the class four basic questions and picks out key words in responses for his flipchart. The questions are:

   - Name some important ground rules for working in a group

   - What is the leader's role?

   - What are the team members' roles?

   - Why are all group roles important to the group working as a team? (10 minutes)

2   Until now Mr Barrington has kept hidden the following six objects which he now produces: shaving mirror, fishing tackle, food hamper, mosquito net, large plastic sheet, large can of water.

   He explains that the group is to imagine they are in a sinking yacht in the Indian Ocean and must convert to an inflatable life-raft. You are the crew and you are to list the objects in order of importance. (10 minutes)

3   The groups have been told that they have just 20 minutes for this task and will need to give a full account of their decisions before the end of the lesson. The first thing is to vote for a leader, a secretary and a spokesperson. (20 minutes)

4   Jill quietly asks Megan whether she wants one of the three positions up for election. She emphatically does not. On the other hand, she is clearly keen on one of the boys in the group (something Jill had never noticed before). In their preliminary discussion, Megan suggests that being in the Indian Ocean might be important and volunteers to go on the Internet in the IT suite.

5   Jill is somewhat phased by this unexpected development, but decides to 'go with the flow', explaining her decision to Mr Barrington, and wheeling Megan down to the IT suite. Jill insists on a 10-minute limit so that Megan can be back for the end of the discussion.

6   When she does return, Megan makes it clear that she does not agree with the order that the group has virtually decided upon and that they should have waited for the Indian Ocean information. Jill is unsure whether this is a genuine intellectual disagreement or Megan 'being bloody-minded'. Jill asks Megan to explain her reasons for differing and reluctantly she does so in short sentences.

7   The group agrees for one major change – the food hamper to be replaced at the top of the list by the fishing tackle. (25 minutes)

8   Each group present their findings and Mr Barrington compliments everyone on at least managing to remain friends. 'The truth is,' he tells them, 'you can make out a case for almost any order.' (15 minutes)

TA liaison sheet

To Megan's TA

Jill,

Remember that as far as Megan is concerned interacting with the group is more important than solving the problem.

1   Please note and report back to me on how she handles the four questions about 'working together'.

2   Note how she reacts to the task itself (e.g. is she positive?)

3   Does she volunteer for a role? If not, why not?

4   What is your assessment of Megan as a team player?

Steven – Year 9. PSHE/citizenship

Under the non-statutory guidelines 'Developing confidence and responsibility and making the most of their abilities' pupils should be taught 'to respect the differences between people as they develop their own sense of identity'.

'Stevie' is a real charmer – sometimes! He is totally inconsistent: one day he is full of enthusiasm, the next day he is very tricky and he needs to be kept on target. Sometimes the strategy of making him sit at the teacher's desk has been used and it works well, but when he is returned to sit with his friends he resumes his quest for constant attention.

Sometimes he seems lazy – looking for the easy way out, but if the mood is right he can be dynamic and come out with lots of ideas. He finds it hard to work independently and he has a short attention span. No one has high expectations of him and he is not going to prove them wrong.

Some of the other pupils don't like him because he can be a bully. He is a permanent lieutenant for some of the tougher boys and does things to win their approval. There have been instances of petty theft, but these have been attention-seeking (e.g. a shoe in the changing rooms), rather than for monetary value.

Since his mother has begun a relationship with a new partner, there has been a deterioration in behaviour and Steven has also been cautioned by police after stealing from a local DIY store. He has just returned from a suspension for throwing a chair at a teacher which staff suspect was done as a result of a dare.

Support

Steven has not so far had any support allocated exclusively to him, although the school has a fair amount of TA time which it keeps flexible each week in order to give support on an 'as and when' basis. One problem here is that as Steven has not had any 1:1 support, there is not a TA who knows him particularly well. However, John Browning, the former head of a special school, has been the TA with other pupils in classes attended by Steven. He volunteers to help out in this PSHE unit in response to the teacher's call for help.

Background

Well aware of Steven's growing problems (because she is the boy's form tutor) the teacher has wisely foreseen the possibility of Steven sabotaging this particular unit of lessons. She feels that the lack of a secure male in Steven's life is behind many of his problems and is delighted that John has volunteered as TA for this unit.

The term's work is taken from 'Active Citizenship: a teaching toolkit', a resource which was developed in-school in Battersea. This particular unit entitled 'Identifying values' works from the basis that pupils cannot examine values in the wider world until they have considered their own.

Last week the class was given an A4 sheet with a spider diagram on it. At the centre of the spider was the question 'What is important to me?' with 12 legs radiating outwards from it so that pupils could register their own concerns. Anticipating some immature responses, the teacher went carefully over the sheet before releasing it, looking at how one had been filled in from an earlier group (anonymously, of course). The sheets had been collected at the end of the lesson and Steven had given responses like 'getting out of this dump', 'surfing in Australia', 'riding a trials bike' (he doesn't have one). The sheet has lots of doodles and scruffy ink marks on it too.

Objectives for this lesson
Pupils will:

- consider positive human values and relate them to pupils' individual values

Objectives for Steven
Steven will:

- stay on task and contribute positively to the lesson

Activities

1 The 'What's important to me?' sheets from the previous week are returned. Each one has been carefully annotated by the teacher, using only questioning and positive comments (including Steven's). The teacher has previously spoken to three pupils about reviewing their work publicly. Having selected the pupils carefully, she proceeds to share their comments and her responses with the class. (10 minutes)

2 The class is divided into five groups of five or six pupils, bringing together as far as possible pupils with similar important concerns but taking care to keep a gender mix. Individually they are given a new sheet to complete, headed 'My future' with a time deadline of 10 minutes. They are to give four responses:

   - my ambition for the future
   - the most positive thing that has ever happened to me
   - what I hope to be doing when I am 30
   - what I hope people will say about me after I have died

3 John, the TA, works with Steven's group rather than Steven. He moves round making constructive comment. When Steven fills in 'being born' under 'most positive thing' he questions him about friendships, holidays, journeys, possessions, then moves on to another pupil. (15 minutes)

4   The teacher announces that each group is now to review the four statements, starting with 'My ambition for the future'. Each pupil is to answer his/her peers for each statement:

- Is it sincere?

- Is it realistic?

- What values does it show? (e.g. money, job, love, possessions, travel, family, fame, etc.) (20 minutes)

John sits in on the group to ensure it keeps its focus.

5   Plenary. Whole class discussion in circle formation with teacher asking pupils how we recognise sincerity, what makes an ambition/hope realistic and (by reference to celebrities) how we (often unwittingly) reveal our values. No definitive statements from teacher, only questions. John sits opposite Steven and surreptitiously notes his responses for follow-up talk with teacher afterwards. (15–20 minutes)

Individual Education Plans

INDIVIDUAL EDUCATION PLAN: ASHRAF

Name: Ashraf Year: 8 Stage: 3	Start date: Review date: IEP no:	Area of concern: SLD Strengths: co-operative Support: TA 1:1
Targets: 1 To discuss with at least one other pupil 2 To show awareness of lesson topic 3 To be actively involved in lesson at least 2x a day	Strategies for use in class: 1 Constant use of first name by teacher 2 Notes for learning diary maintained by TA and written up co-operatively at end of day 3 Topic clearly enunciated at start of lesson and frequently referred to 4 TA regularly asks Ashraf his opinion on how the lesson is going (for whole class)	Role of parent(s) carer(s) 1 Daily check work on laptop 2 Ask Ashraf about classmates 3 Be informed what topics Ashraf will be learning about
Success criteria: 1 Remembering the names of at least 3 pupils per lesson 2 List of topics in daily learning diary 3 List of tasks undertaken in learning diary	Resources: 1 Learning diary (in laptop format for Ashraf) 2 Room seating plan for Ashraf and TA 3 Guidelines for staff	Agreed by: SENCO: Parent(s): Pupil: Date:

INDIVIDUAL EDUCATION PLAN: STEVEN

Name: Steven Year: 9 Stage: 2	Start date: Review date: IEP no:	Area of concern: EBD Strengths: can by dynamic; lots of ideas if mood is right Support: as and when needed
Targets: 1 To remain in his seat for the majority of the lesson. 2 To show no aggression towards other pupils. 3 To leave each lesson with something positive achieved. 4 To produce written work independently at least three times a week.	Strategies for use in class: 1 Steven's planner to have a section in which he records each day's best achievement. 2 John Browning to be made available for a 10-minute meeting with Steven at the end of each day. 3 Seat him near the front of the class and away from pupils with whom he reacts negatively. 4 Class seating plan established for each lesson. 5 A calm but assertive demand for Steven to return to his seat when he wanders. 6 Plenty of praise when Steven has a successful day/lesson. 7 As many lessons as possible to have a variety of activities.	Role of parent(s) carer(s) 1 To be completely *au fait* with these targets. 2 Calm routines in the morning before school. 3. Agreement to inform school regularly of any changes to Steven's life outside school.
Success criteria: 1 To measure his targets one day at a time. When he can achieve 1, 2 and 3 in one day, then look to manage them for a second day and so on. 2 Contact with his peers revealing an improved social standing. 3 An improvement in presentation and quality in work in exercise books. 4 Greater personal accountability for his day-to-day behaviour.	Resources: 1 Guidelines for all staff provided. 2 Appropriate stationery arrangements for Steven to record achievement. 3 John Browning to be made available for last 10 minutes of each day (at least). 4 Available area for 'time out' if need arises.	Agreed by: SENCO: Parent(s): Pupil: Date:

INDIVIDUAL EDUCATION PLAN: MEGAN

Name: Megan Year: 10 Stage: 3	Start date: Review date: IEP no:	Area of concern: Anti-social behaviour, poor self-control Strengths: Intelligent, sensitive Support: Full-time
Targets: 1 To take an active role when working in a group learning situation. 2 To show the leadership qualities which she undoubtedly possesses. 3 To contain her temper, in particular with members of staff with whom she works closely. 4 To fulfil her homework obligations.	**Strategies for use in class:** 1 At a quick signal from Megan, her TA will remove her from the lesson and take her to a 'time-out' room. . 2 Time set aside at lunchtime for Megan to do her homework *when she wants to*. 3 Every Thursday night her special minibus replaced by a late taxi so that she can attend homework club. 4 Subject teachers ensure that Megan is asked plenty of questions in class. 5 Daily review by TA to include a consideration of where Megan was/could have been more positive/proactive.	**Role of parent(s) carer(s)** 1 Calm routines in the morning before school. 2 Closer involvement with homework routines. 3 Agreed time for phone calls from Meagan's TA on a need basis. 4 To discuss temper loss with Megan when it occurs at home.
Success criteria: 1 To succeed with holding her temper one day at a time. When she has managed one day, then to target two consecutive days. 2 To receive acknowledgement in her planner (from her TA or the subject teacher) that she has shown leadership potential at least three times a week. 3 That she leaves the room immediately when she feels things getting 'too much'. 4 Another one day at a time approach. First one night's full homework completed, then to target two and so on.	**Resources:** 1 'Time-out' room. 2 Guidelines for all staff provided. 3 Voluntary staff roster for helping Megan with lunchtime homework. 4 Training of Megan's TA by suitable staff re positive and proactive approaches.	**Agreed by:** SENCO: Parent(s): Pupil: Date:

Sample Care Action Plan

No Further Action ☐
Continuing ☐

Date

Sent for signature ☐
Sent to client ☐
Sent to carer ☐
Other ☐

LEARNING DISABILITY SERVICE – TEL: 0

CARE/ACTION PLAN – OUTCOME MEASURE

Client's Name	John White	Date of Birth	1/1/91	Care Plan No	2	File Number	1795
Team Member	Graham Brown	Profession	Acting Clinical Manager		Date of Care/Action Plan		02/03/03

Client's Priorities/Long Term Objectives:
needs assistance in developing a greater understanding of his own condition, how this impacts upon his behaviour and how he can develop management strategies for this.

Initial Evaluation	Goal	Action	Re-Evaluation Outcome
John presents with a mild/moderate learning disability and severe autism. Historically John's behaviour has presented as aggression towards others and damage to property. His move to South School has had a positive effect upon his behaviour. He continues to present as being very anxious with low self esteem, having the awareness that he is very different from other youngsters of his own age.	To help John take more control of his behavioural outbursts. To assist all those who work or care for John to develop a greater understanding of autism in general and also the specific needs of John.	Liaison within family home, school and with Social Services. Direct 1:1 work with John working on the 'I am special' package/anger management.	(PTO for more space) Carer's Input Maximum ☐ Occasional ☐ Minimal ☐ Not Relevant ☐ Goal Exceeded ☐ Goal Achieved ☐ Goal Partially Achieved ☐ Goal Not Achieved ☐
Date of Action	07.03.03	Date of Re-Evaluation	September 2003

PUPIL IEP TARGETS: John White

TARGET 1: To settle in successfully to South School

MY ACTION PLAN

- Remember all my equipment
- Find my way around school successfully
- Understand my timetable
- Use my homework diary correctly

TARGET 2: To avoid losing my temper

MY ACTION PLAN

- Ask for help with my work when I need it
- Say only nice things to other people
- Walk away from anyone attempting to wind me up
- If I feel cross go to GR4 to find help
- Discuss any problems with Daniel and listen to his advice

TARGET 3: Improve my literacy and numeracy skills

MY ACTION PLAN

- Attend extra tuition sessions in spelling and reading
- Score above 50% in a spelling test on words I have tried to learn
- Achieve the maths target set for me by my teacher

Evaluation of progress   Subject.................................. Teacher..................................

Academic progress

Behaviour

Relationship with other pupils

Relationship with adults

PARENTAL INVOLVEMENT

- Weekly contact will be made by D. *Black*
  Mr and Mrs *White* will make arrangements to come into school to meet Mr *Green* and Mr *Grey*

MONITORING ARRANGEMENTS

- Daily by form tutor and PSA

- Weekly, or more frequently if necessary, by SEN Department

REVIEW DATE: 23/09/02

Signed

.... Key Worker

Date: ....

EVALUATION by Pupil and Key Worker

- Mr & Mrs White came into school to meet-
  her to establish personal contact and to
  make for easier relationships if
  John becomes involved in confrontations
  in school — as opposed to standard letters
  going home.

INDIVIDUAL EDUCATION PLAN

NAME: *John White*   DOB: *1/1/91*   FORM: STAGE: 1 2③

PROGRESS:

- John has responded well to recent additional classroom support in his primary school

- He enjoys and uses computers well

- Some small steps of progress have been made recently in the development of his literacy skills

- He has been very positive about having a fresh start in a school where he is not known to other pupils

DIFFICULTIES:

- Social communication difficulties with his peers

- Unpredicatable and challenging behaviour

- Literacy skills remain very weak

- Spelling and handwriting skills are particularly weak

- Difficulties with fine motor skills

OBJECTIVES:

- Improve social communication skills

- Improve self control and anger management

- Improve literacy and numeracy skills.

STAFF ACTION PLAN:

- *John* needs a great deal of direct encouragement from adults in the classroom. His last classteacher managed to establish a good relationship with him by being quietly persistent and giving him small responsibilities in the classroom.

- Instructions may need to be given to him individually and step by step.

- Success however small needs to be recognised.

- If he does not comply with any instructions please remind calmly and firmly. He does not react well to shouts or raised voices.

- Persistent failure to follow instruction will need a quiet 'one to one' conversation with him to highlight the expectations for the behaviour of pupils in secondary school.

- In the case of any outburst call the member of SMT on call who will collect him for a period of 'time out'.

ADDITIONAL ARRANGEMENTS

- Access where appropriate to small group teaching for additional literacy tuition – R. Gold

- Regular review of social skills

- Access to time out facilities in Learning Support room or with member of SMT on call

- Full time access to PSA support

- Anger management training – learning to cope with pupil provocation – Behaviour Support teacher

- Regular contact with parents

Assisting TA Input in a Citizenship Discussion Lesson

Subject

Are pupils in favour of everyone carrying an ID card?

Introduction

Outline different kinds of identity card and give examples of societies which already use them.

Class discussion (Order of issues):

1   What are the different purposes they can be used for?

2   Why are some people in favour of carrying them?

3   Why are some people against carrying them?

4   What would happen if you lost one or had it stolen?

5   Now decide whether YOU are in favour of or against carrying cards.

I could take a photocopy of my lesson notes (particularly with regard to point 1) if you wanted advance information.

NB: I shall be pushing all pupils to make a decision on the basis of the discussion because how we weigh up evidence is one of my main teaching and learning points.

References

Bryson, B. (1990) *Mother Tongue.* London: Penguin.

Dethridge, T. and Dethridge, M. (2002) *Literacy Through Symbols.* London: David Fulton Publishers.

DfEE/QCA (1999) *The National Curriculum Handbook for Secondary Teachers in England and Wales.* QCA/99/458.

Fox, G. (1993) *A Handbook for Special Needs Assistants: Working in Partnership with Teachers.* Oxford: David Fulton Publishers.

Ofsted (2001) *Inspecting Subjects 11-16 – New Developments in the Secondary Curriculum with guidance on self-evaluation.* HMI 262.

Oliver, I. (2000) *Ready to Go: Ideas for PSHE (KS2).* London: Scholastic.

QCA (2001) *Planning, teaching and assessing the curriculum for pupils with learning difficulties: PSHE and citizenship.* QCA/01/749.

QCA (2001) *Citizenship: A scheme of work for Key Stage 3.* QCA/01/776.

Further Reading

Bailey, R. (ed.) (2000) *Teaching Values and Citizenship Across the Curriculum.* London: Kogan Page.

Britton, F. (2000) *Active Citizenship (a teaching toolkit).* London: Hodder & Stoughton/CSV.

Combes, A. S. (2001) *21st Century Citizen: Key Stage 3.* Filey: Cable Educational.

Hicks, D. (2001) *Citizenship for the Future.* WWF-UK.

Mosley, J. and Tew, M. (1999) *Quality Circle Time in Secondary School.* London: David Fulton Publishers.

Osborne, E. and Yates, S. (2001) *Citizenship and PSHE.* Dunstable: Folens.

Potter, J. (2002) *Active Citizenship in Schools.* London: Kogan Page/CSV.

Rowe, D. (2001) *Introducing Citizenship (A Handbook for Primary Schools).* London: A & C Black.

Turner, D. and Baker, P. (2000) *Developing Citizenship in Secondary Schools.* London: Kogan Page.

Watkinson, A. (2002) *Assisting Learning and Supporting Teaching.* London: David Fulton Publishers.